PRO SHOOTING SECRETS

THE ONLY SHOOTING SYSTEM
THAT UNLOCKS THE HIDDEN TRUTH
BEHIND TODAY'S GREATEST SHOOTERS

Paul Hoover

Founder of the Pro Shot Shooting System

www.proshotsystem.com

Printed in the United States of America

PRO SHOOTING SECRETS

This book is a work of non-fiction.

Third Edition 2012

ISBN: 1599160277

Dedicated to the developing shooter and to all
my students and players who have
inspired me with their dedication,
discipline, and vision

AUTHOR'S NOTE:

Please note that Pro Shooting Secrets is a shooting system for all ages and for both genders. For easier reading comprehension, I have wrote using the male pronoun throughout the text. As you continue reading further you will discover that I use the pronoun "he" instead of "he/she." This is done only to simplify the reading.

TABLE OF CONTENTS

THE JOURNEY TO SHOOTING PERFECTION

For 20 years I searched for the truth—the truth for shooting perfection. This was a journey few basketball coaches have ever taken. Some might call it a passion and others would believe it's much closer to an obsession. As I dwelled more into the art of shooting, many of my coaching friends would mock my enthusiasm for this basketball discipline.

In my playing days I was a very average shooter at best. Reflecting back now I realize that I was a puppet controlled by my coaches. What they told me to do, I always did. I never questioned anything no matter how uncomfortable the shot became. When I first picked up the whistle late in my teens and began my coaching career, I would teach my players these same flawed concepts that I was originally taught. For the next few years my teams were just like every other squad full of "brick layers." And then I saw the light...

THE FIRST STEP: KNOWLEDGE

In 1985, at age 20, I landed a job at one of the most prestigious high school basketball programs on the west coast, Mater Dei in Santa Ana, California. Mater Dei doesn't just win games—they collect state banners. It was during my Mater Dei coaching stint that I was introduced to Des Flood. Des was a shooting coach who worked from his backyard in nearby Garden Grove. Every weekend I drove players to Des for private shooting instruction. Des was a nationally renowned shooting instructor. His credits included training the men's basketball programs at Stanford and Iowa Universities in the art of shooting.

I was amazed at the impact each player had with Des's mentoring. Improvement in every shooter was immediate and noticeable. In a way, it was as if he was playing God since the results were instantaneous and dramatic. I was astounded that a coach could make so much of a difference in such a short period of time.

Des Flood had a tremendous influence in my life. Sadly, I don't believe he ever understood the true significance that his knowledge and friendship had on me. Des passed away in 1995 of a heart attack before I got the chance to express my true gratitude for his mentoring. Not a day goes by that I don't think of him first and foremost as a friend and secondly, as a tremendous shooting instructor.

THE SECOND STEP: SPIRITUAL

Similar to Don Quixote who chased windmills, for the next two decades I continued chasing jump shots in my quest of finding answers. I would take Des Flood's teachings and use that as my shooting base. As I dwelled more and more into shooting techniques, however, I became increasingly aware that the common shooting methods that were being taught by most coaches were not being used by the best shooters at the high school, collegiate and professional levels. I would study the best NBA shooters and ask, "What makes him such a great shooter?" Most coaching friends that I would speak with would explain to me, "The reason that player is such a great shooter is simply because he practices a lot." This explanation was just too simple for me to accept. That would be like saying an accomplished actor is that way simply because he acts a lot.

As I continued teaching young athletes to shoot, I discovered few athletes truly understand what mental focusing is all about. They would stare at the basket and fail to recognize what their body was actually doing in the process. For poor shooters, their mind shuts down while shooting a basketball. With out mental feedback, the body because a series of seizures, spasms and off balanced movements. Soon I realized that for accurate shooting, the mind and body are very similar to the Zen approach of the Yin and the Yang. Without one, the other fails to exist. Many coaches tell their players, "Focus only on the rim." The player stares at the rim only to proceed with miss after miss. Focusing on the body with mental feedback, on the other hand, allows the player to control their shot while staying tension free.

Understanding fully the notion of the mind working with the body, I then had to discover the body's workings when shooting a basketball. In October, 2005, I designed the Pro Shot Shooting System. Pro Shot is a biomechanically system that defines the body working together with focus and concentration to create a rhythmic and fluidic shot that is accurate and quick. The Pro Shot System was designed through studying and speaking with many of the top shooters and trainers in the world.

THE THIRD STEP: INFORM AND BELIEVE

"When the highest type of men hear Tao,
They diligently practice it.
When the average type of men hear Tao,
They half believe it.
When the lowest type of men hear Tao,
They laugh heartily at it."
Lao Tzu
Chinese Philosopher

Having successfully completed my mission to build the ultimate shooting program, my final journey is to spread the word of the Pro Shot System across the United States and beyond. You are about to read the most revolutionary and comprehensive shooting book ever written. There has never been a shooting book that depicts the mental, physical and emotional side like Pro Shooting Secrets. My ultimate goal is to change the poor shooting that I see too often throughout my travels.

One of my favorite athletes is Dick Fosbury. Only a few people know this name outside of track and field. What Fosbury did, however, was to completely revolutionize an entire sport. As a young high jumper in the early 60's, Fosbury had difficulty mastering the standard "Straddle" technique. He began experimenting with an approach to the bar with his back to it, and he jumped in a scissors motion bringing him over the bar backwards. The technique was christened the "Fosbury Flop" by a Medford, Oregon sports reporter. A few years later the "Fosbury Flop" became world

renown when Fosbury won a high jump gold medal in the 1968 Mexico City Olympics.

At first there were critics to Fosbury's unusual techniques. "Kids imitate champions," commented USA Olympic coach Payton Jordan soon after Fosbury won the gold medal, "If they try to imitate Fosbury, he will wipe out an entire generation of high jumpers because they will all have broken necks." Of course this did not occur. The high jumpers that followed Fosbury didn't break their necks, but instead began breaking world records. After the "Fosbury Flop" was universally adopted, the average rate of improvement to the sport was two times greater than before. In short, Dick Fosbury changed high jumping forever.

With any change, there are always those who have a difficult time accepting and believing. "The problem with something revolutionary like that was that most of the elite athletes had invested so much time in their technique and movements that they didn't want to give it up, so they stuck with what they knew," Fosbury said. When he won the gold in 1968, Fosbury was the only one implementing the "Flop" technique. Within a few years after his gold medal performance, every top high jumper at the international level was successfully using his technique. Similar to Fosbury, I seek to change the way shooting is currently viewed.

In this book, I have assembled fifteen years of observations, experiences, and ideas concerning proper shooting. I hope this book will be an easy and enjoyable read for everyone: from the young and eager athlete to the most sophisticated coach. Please note that I am a big a fan of both quotes and movie lines. Throughout Pro Shooting Secrets you will discover many scenes and quotes from the motion picture industry that will correlate training and shooting which will further enhance my points.

When I was the director of the Southern California Basketball Academy, I would take a few minutes during each session to speak to my students about different aspects of the game. After awhile, the Academy members called these discussions "Story time" (some players referred to them as sermons). I have continued this throughout Pro Shooting Secrets to help illustrate the System. Many of these stories come directly from my coaching experience. Some are chronicled from stories that I have read while others have come from talking to my fellow coaches.

I hope that everyone enjoys Pro Shooting and discovers that these shooting concepts will change how each player, parent, and coach views the art of shooting.

SECTION I:

SHOOTING IMPORTANCE

"He wins who scores more points than his opponents in basketball, and shooting is the backbone of the game."

Bill Sharman
From the book, "Sharman on Basketball Shooting"

1. STATE OF SHOOTING

The most important fundamental skill a basketball player can possess is the ability to accurately shoot. Proper shooting can often make the difference between a player becoming successful or wallowing in obscure mediocrity. Shooting can take teams with average athletic skill and turn them into championship contenders.

Unfortunately, most of today's players don't understand the importance of accurate shooting. All you have to do is look at the best scorers in the NBA and you will discover that all of these players are good to excellent shooters.

If you look at the NBA teams that are always contending for an NBA championship you will notice that they are all excellent shooting squads formed more on "swish" than on "flash." The same thing can be said about college teams that make a run at the NCAA crown.

Many young players see basketball as an athletic game that's all about dunking and displaying "And One Mix Tape" moves. Yes, the art of shooting is viably suffering throughout in North America.

Sports Illustrated understood the shooting problem in the mid-90's when they ran an article and asked: "Where have all the shooters gone?" Since this article, shooting has actually taken a turn for the worse. These days the old adage, "charity stripe," means giving away your opportunities instead of cashing them in.

THE JUMPER VANISHES FROM AMERICA

"I don't think anyone can shoot. It's because of what I call the ESPNization of the game. How do you get on ESPN highlights? You make some giant move. They don't show a guy hitting 8-of-10 shots from 20 feet. That's not news. What's news is the guy that drives the middle, flips around in the air and tosses it up or does a giant dunk. That's what they put on TV. So kids are, 'Well, that's what I want to do.' And they don't put in time shooting."

Bill Bradley

Senator and Basketball Hall of Fame Player

The United States appears to have forgotten how important shooting the ball can actually be. There are a few reasons behind this neglect. First and foremost, shooting is seldom highlighted on ESPN and Fox sports broadcasts. What seems to make the highlight reels are the endless clips of slam-dunks. Having coached at both inner-city and wealthy high schools, it's amazing how many of my players would talk about a Jordan or Kobe dunk from the night before. The King of Air could have made five three pointers in that same game, yet it would be that one amazing dunk that most young players remembered the most and wanted to discuss.

The jump shot has given us many unforgettable memories and moments. While the slam-dunk continues to be more popular, the jump shot is what wins games and determines championships. Think about how many games you have watched that have been won in the last ten seconds. How many were won by a shot (whether it's a jumper or a free throw) and how many were won by a slam-dunk? I have been involved with basketball for 25 years and have seen only a few games decided in the last seconds by a dunk. During this time, however, I have witnessed thousands of games won by a single shot. It's truly a no brainer—the shot wins every time.

IT MUST BE THE SHOES

Shoe companies don't appear to care about these last minute shooting heroics. In their boardrooms, the most often used word appears to be DUNK. Since the early 80's, shoe companies have spent multi-millions marketing the dunk. We have been besieged by dunk posters, dunk television ads, and dunk action figures. Dunks— dunks—dunks—everywhere there are dunks. But where are the jump shots? The shoe companies and the media have "programmed" this generation to believe basketball is all about the dunk.

"A Jump shot will get you...
A shoe deal
A supermodel
A posse
A screen test
A new car
A big house
A jet plane
A book deal
A recording contract

But none of these things will get you a jump shot."
Reebok Commercial
June 2005

In June 2005 Reebok finally saw the light and decided to embrace the jump shot. Reebok became the first shoe company to focus a television commercial entirely on shooting. The 30 second commercial explained the perks that a great shooter receives. I hope Reebok will be a trendsetter and other shoes companies will follow by focusing more on shooting and less on dunking. This would definitely give basketball a great needed boost of adrenaline. But don't bet on it.

BASKETBALL GOES GLOBAL

In the mid 1990's, there were only a handful of NBA players born outside of the United States. The best players in the world were American and professional scouts and coaches fully understood this as they roamed from college to college looking for their needs. Times have changed. At the beginning of the 2004/2005 season, the Utah Jazz had half of their roster players born outside of the United States. Eighty percent of the starting lineup for the 2005 World Champion San Antonio Spurs were foreign born.

Currently, 33% of NBA players are foreign born. The reason for this influx of foreign players is that NBA coaches and general managers want players with shooting ability and overall offensive skills. They are no longer looking for athletic players that lack shooting accuracy.

JUMPSHOT 101

"I am familiar with the fact that you are going to ignore this particular problem until it swims up and bites you on the ass!"
Richard Dreyfuss as Hooper
From the Motion Picture, "Jaws"

Throughout European countries, coaches and players study shooting. In these countries there is a greater emphasis on becoming an accurate shooter than there is in the United States. If you play basketball in Lithuania, for example, you are expected to be a good shooter even if you're the tallest player on your team. In the United States, in contrast, coaches are surprised when they find one pure shooter on a team because it's such a rare commodity.

The problem is that most players and coaches in North America really have limited understanding of proper shooting techniques. I would estimate that 90% of what is being taught n regards to shooting is actually incorrect information.

In some ways, having a good jump shot in the new millennium has become outdated and uncool. It's almost as if an accurate shot is Americana from the distant past—Norman Rockwell paints: "Alone in a Gym." Yes, the Jimmy Chickwoods (the pure shooter from the motion picture, "Hoosiers" that honed his basketball talents on a dirt surface) have become few and far between. Young players often fail to realize that it takes a great amount of luck to be 6'10" (this being the luck of being born to the right parents).

It also takes luck (or good genes) to be blessed with having long arms. Anyone can become a shooter, however. There is no luck associated with shooting, only skill combined with disciplined training. Shooting is for everyone, no matter what the player's height, weight, or genetic makeup may be. All it takes to be a great shooter is technique, practice, discipline, focus and patience. If a player displays these qualities on a daily basis, his shot will improve and success in his overall offensive game will soon follow.

Unfortunately, many younger players (and a few older ones as well) don't fully understand how accurate shooting can benefit their game. Often times I am taken back how naive players can be. On January 22, 2006, Kobe Bryant scored 81 points against the Toronto Raptors. The 81 points was the second highest total in one game in NBA history. But how many points were off the dunk? I once had a young player in Illinois respond, "He scored half of the 81." In reality, Kobe only scored 2 baskets (and one was a break-away) off the dunk. Players that respond back with a high number of dunk points are usually the ones most infatuated by the dunk. These are the same players that fail to realize the importance of shooting accurately.

"REALITY BITES"

During the late 90's, I coached two brothers, Jamaal and Jason Taylor. Jamaal was one of the easiest players that I have coached (you will read more about him regarding the Off Hand). Everything that I ever told him to do, he did. Jamaal never fought my instruction and he was always open-minded. His shooting improvement was quite startling. In a two-year span he went from making zero three-pointers on his junior varsity team to becoming the leading varsity three point shooter in Orange County (92 successful makes his senior season). He transformed from an athlete with virtually no jump shot to a quick and deadly shooter.

Jamaal's younger brother, Jason, was a completely different story. Jason was a quick point guard with decent ballhandling skills. For the most part, Jason resisted my instruction throughout the two years that I trained him. He didn't believe shooting was important and often neglected to practice this skill. Jason hated change and shunned any new methods I attempted to employ. I couldn't understand why he wasn't being open-minded to my instruction. After all, couldn't he see the great progress that his brother was making right before his eyes?

Unfortunately, Jason's shooting improved very little. Still I continued working with him hoping there would one day be a breakthrough. As fate would have it, I was coaching the boys' basketball team at Santa Ana Valley High School and Jason's team, Canyon High School, happened to be in the same league. We played Canyon twice and came out victorious both times by one and two points respectively. In the long run, my sharp shooting team won a Century League Championship with a 9-1mark. Canyon's team meanwhile finished with a 7-3 record and third place in the league.

One day when I was getting nowhere with Jason I finally asked him, "I have a question—is shooting important to you?"

"It's okay. But my real skill is dribbling."

"Do you know what you shot from the three point line when we played you?" I asked.

Because I had a manager video record all of our games, I knew exactly what his shooting numbers were. Jason shook his head. "You were 0-11 from behind the arch. That's 0-6 the first game and 0-5 the second game. Now think about this. If you go 1-6 in the first game and 1-5 in the second, you would have beaten us both times. And now we're third place and Canyon wins the league championship."

Jason looked at me with an expression that said, 'I am an idiot.' Because Jason had failed to understand that shooting is crucial in a player's overall game, he had cost his team a chance for a Century League Championship. REALITY BITES!

YOU MUST BECOME A SHOOTER!

One of the greatest "misconceptions" taught by coaches is that there are five positions in basketball. In reality, there are really only four true positions. Before you have me committed to the nearest mental institution, let me fully explain. The five basketball positions that we are accustomed to include: point guard, shooting guard or off guard, small forward, power forward, and post/center. If you look at most successful teams, however, there are actually only four true positions. These four positions are as follows:

- **The Point Guard**. This is the leader, the general, the player that sets up the offense. This is the player with lightning fast ballhandling and outstanding passing skills. Usually this player is handed a basketball as soon as he comes out of the womb. Five percent of all players fall into this category.

- **The Big Man.** This is the player in the middle that takes up space. Al McGuire, former Marquette coach, used to call this position the "aircraft carrier." In college, these players are usually 6'9" and taller. In high school the true big man is usually 6'6" and taller. These are players that usually have "tall" genes. If your parents are both 5'4" chances are pretty decent you will not be in this category. Five percent of all players fall into this category.

- **The Great Athlete.** This player usually is a versatile athlete that can play on the perimeter and can cut effectively to the basket. Usually the great athlete is notoriously aggressive at both ends of the floor. Their pure athleticism and hard-nosed play often times makes up for a lack of fundamental basketball skills. These players can vary in height but are usually known as "wing" players. Five percent of all players fall into this category.

- **The Shooter**. This is the guy that can effectively launch from the "cheap seats." This rare player is usually known as a zone buster and has ice water in his veins. The shooter is known to consistently hit the backbreaking shots against the opposition. These players truly make the difference in a game. Five percent of all players fall into this category.

As you may have already discovered, if you add up the entire percentages from these four positions it only totals 20%. So, what positions do the other 80% of all players fall into? Often times they are in the infamous position called "left out" as in they are on the team, but left out of the coach's plans. These are the players that constantly mumble, "Coach doesn't like me." In a way, that player is absolutely correct. A coach doesn't like this type of player because he can't do anything for the team. Any coach will always favor players with ability and skill because they produce the stuff that wins games. When you have little to give a coach, he normally has little to give you in return.

A player in that 80% group is lucky if he is in the "left out" position because there is an excellent chance that he may get cut. This is the most dreaded word in all of sports next to "career ending injury." What I find amusing is the player who gets cut, continues to do the same form of training on his own, then returns the following year only to be cut again. He basically got cut because he wasn't good enough, and now he's doing exactly the same training again. Unless that player has grown six inches, can he really expect to make the team by doing the same old tired things?

Please understand that when a player is a great shooter and falls into one of the other three categories, that player will usually become a superstar. If you look at Kobe Bryant, for example, he is first and foremost a great athlete who has made himself into an excellent shooter. Many of the top scorers in the league at the off guard and small forward positions (Carmelo Anthony, Danny Granger, Dwyane Wade) are great athletes as well as terrific shooters.

WHO AM I?

Here's a situation that occurs often in youth basketball across America. A player is a standout on the basketball court because he is naturally strong and tall at a young age (4th-8th grades). This player excels on his team because he can overpower weaker and smaller opponents. As this player gets closer to high school, his growth pattern begins to slow down while everyone else seems to catch up and eventually passes that player in bulk and height. This player has played the post position all of his life and for this reason he has limited perimeter and shooting skills. Because he has always played hard and aggressively, he has paid little attention to the finesse aspects of the game, including shooting. This player should be focusing on shooting the most since he no longer has a position and yet, it can be like pulling teeth to get him into a gym to work on his shooting skills. He often fails to understand the importance that shooting must have in his life, and for this reason this player will sit on the bench in high school or will quit the game to focus on another sport where he can better use his physical talents (usually football or wrestling).

"THE PLAYER WITHOUT A POSITION"

In the spring of 2003 I was introduced to Ryan Fleming, a 6'4" high school junior from Pasadena, California. Ryan had just transferred from a large Catholic high school, Loyola, to a much smaller one, St. Francis, hoping he could standout in his senior season.

Ryan had excellent basketball genes. His father had played for the University of Dayton and later for a season backing up Pete Maravich with the Atlanta Hawks in the early 70's. His uncle had played at Notre Dame and his grandfather played with George Mikan and the Minneapolis Lakers. The Flemings definitely had basketball blood running through their family tree.

When I first met Ryan, I explained to him my four-position theory and then put him through a series of questions. "Are you a point guard?"

He chuckled, "No way."

"What about a big man?"

"I've played it, but that's not my true position," Ryan responded.

"What about a great athlete? Are you a great athlete?"

Ryan looked at me as if I was from outer space. Once again he laughed. "I wish."

"Ryan, you're not a big man, you're not a point guard, and you say you are not a great athlete. That means you have to become a shooter. If you aren't a shooter, there's really no place for you in this game," I explained. "Has anyone ever told you this?"

"No." Ryan had been through various coaches and trainers throughout Southern California and no one had ever explained to him the only chance he ever had to become a standout high school player and receive a collegiate scholarship was to develop into a shooter. I was honestly stunned by his answer. If Ryan would have understood five years earlier that he had to become a shooter, he would have had college coaches lining up on his doorstep. Unfortunately, because no coach had ever told him this, he was a mediocre player with average skills.

BASKETBALL IS A SIMPLE GAME

While my team is warming up before a game, I generally watch the other team shoot. What I'm looking for are the players that are "tickling the twines." In other words, I'm trying to identify who the other team's shooters are before tip-off. Here's what I've discovered in all my years coaching from the fourth grade level through the professional ranks—the players who constantly stand on the perimeter during warm-ups and swish their shots don't normally sit on the bench during the game.

If you can shoot, you will play. It's that simple! Of course there can be overriding factors such as when a player becomes suspended, is apathetic, or lazy. Generally, if you have a good attitude and can accurately shoot, you will see very little bench time. If players understood the significance of having a good shot and understand that shooters get to play, you would suddenly see more players focus on the disciplines of shooting, combined with practice, practice, and more practice.

Unfortunately, for many players having a good jump shot is near the bottom of their basketball skills totem pole of overall importance. I often hear about players that train with running coaches, but at the same time have limited shooting skills.

Give me a player that can shoot the ball over a fast athlete who has a problem putting the ball in the basket, and I will beat you every single time. Running correctly is a good skill to have; being fast helps; and jumping high is an additional plus. Shooting the ball accurately, however, is the most important fundamental in all of basketball.

ARE YOU A GREAT SHOOTER?

"You ever done anything with somebody that has no concept of himself. I play ball with these guys at the Y in LA. They will miss every shot and it's as if every shot is this individual phenomenon. It's like—'Ah damn!' 'Jeez!' Hey, maybe you just can't shoot. Did it ever occur to you that you just can't shoot. That maybe you just stink."
Dom Irrera
Comedian

One of the most amusing things to see is a player with no concept of good shooting. He will stand out by the three-point line during practice and miss shot after shot. Occasionally, there may be a rare make scattered among the shots which often leads the player to remark, "I'm getting hot!" Of course that individual will miss another 5-10 shots before finally making another shot. The player simply refuses to realize that this is not good at shooting.

When speaking at camps, I will ask the players, "Raise your hand if you think you're a great shooter." Normally, over half of the hands rise. Then I explain, "My idea of a great shooter is a player that will take ten shots from the three point line and make 8 or 9 shots when practicing alone. How many players here can do that?" The once eager hands normally all come down at this point.

Usually there is the one overconfident player that will continue raising his hand claiming to be the next Ray Allen. I will bring that player out and have him attempt 10 three point shots. On average he will make 1-3 of these three pointers. This "tough love" isn't breaking the players' spirit, but instead it's bringing him back to the reality that his shot desperately needs work and attention.

The following table helps to understand the difference between a good and a poor shooter. This is based around high school and collegiate players and what they make when shooting around the arc when rested.

- Great Shooters will make 8-10/10
- Good Shooters will make 7/10
- Average Shooters will make 6/10
- Below Average Shooters will make 4-5/10
- Poor Shooters will make 0-3/10

THE GAME FORMULA

Want to see what your shooting percentage will be in a game? Understand that you are normally half as effective in a game as you are when practicing alone. This usually occurs because of fatigue, too much tension, and the anxiety and excitement of the game. Try this for yourself. Take ten shots from the three-point line and see how many you make. Now take the makes and multiply by ten, and then divide by two. This is your approximate shooting percentage for a game. For example, say you made eight out of ten shots. If you multiply your makes by 10 (8 x 10) you get 80 and when you divide this number by two, you become a 40% three-point shooter. Please note that anything below 30% is a player that a coach doesn't want shooting from the perimeter in a game. Again I repeat:

- Great Shooters will make 40-50%
- Good Shooters will make 35%
- Average Shooters will make 30%
- Below Average Shooters will make 25%
- Poor Shooters make 0-20%

CHAPTER 1 WRAP UP:

- Shooting is the most important fundamental skill a basketball player can possess.

- The art of shooting is slowly dying in North America.

- In the United States, corporations and the media have brainwashed our younger generation to believe it's all about the dunk.

- Foreign-born players are infiltrating the NBA in record numbers because they can shoot.

- In European countries, coaches and players study shooting.

- Shooting is for everyone, no matter a player's height, weight or genetic makeup.

- The players that constantly stand on the perimeter during warm-ups and swish shots, don't sit during the game.

- If you can shoot, you will play.

SECTION II:

FIVE COMPONENTS TO CHANGE

**"It is not the strongest of the species that survive,
nor the most intelligent,
but the one most responsive to change."**

Charles Darwin
Naturalist

2. DISCIPLINED PRACTICE

There's an old story about the lost tourist that approaches the classic pianist on a New York street corner and asks him, "How do you get to Carnegie Hall?" The classic pianist replies, "Practice, my good man, practice." Of course basketball and shooting are really no different. How does a basketball player ever get to Madison Square Garden or the Staples Center? The answer always is "Practice, practice, and more practice."

Somehow we have forgotten how great shooters truly become great shooters. Why are Dirk Nowitski and Ray Allen two of the best shooters in the world? It's definitely not by playing Playstation or texting on their phone all day. I have yet to discover a great shooter who seldom practices, and I have also never found a poor shooter who practices in a focused manner every day. Interestingly, focused practice and accurate shooting go hand in hand.

The problem is that we live in an "attention deficit disorder" society. During the past few decades our attention span has been reduced from minutes to seconds. Call it the "MTV generation." Thirty years ago a high school player would shoot alone at a basket for an hour. Ask a player to attempt this today and after only a few minutes his mind will begin to wonder and his overall shot discipline will falter. It used to be that kids went outside and played. If you were a basketball player, you went outdoors and practiced. In fact, if you stayed inside you were generally considered a "freak." Oh, how times have changed!

In my camps and clinics, I always tell players that if your thumb is the strongest part of your body (used the most in texting and video games), chances are you will never be a quality shooter, let alone a good basketball player.

Through my travels talking one-on-one to excellent collegiate and professional shooters, I have noticed that these players normally have a tremendous work-ethic. This work-ethic is a belief that a shooter must shoot everyday, 365 days a year (or somewhere closes to that). In some ways, it's an obsession that the competition is always working harder than they are.

"GREATNESS BY GUILT"

I first met Dylan Rigdon his freshman year (1986) at Mater Dei High School. Dylan played very sparingly as a freshman and joined my sophomore team the following season. Immediately, I saw that he had tremendous potential. Though not very aggressive and slight of build, he was a decent ball handler, a steady passer and a good shooter. Through training hours upon hours in a gym, Dylan made himself into an exceptional shooter. He later played two years at UC Irvine only to transfer to the University of Arizona and participate in the 1994 Final Four. Arizona Head Basketball, Coach Lute Olson, once commented that Dylan is one of the two top shooters he had coached at U of A (the other being Steve Kerr).

Dylan married his longtime girlfriend, Molly Munoz (who happens to be John Wayne's granddaughter) in 2001. I was the only coach at the wedding, held in Newport Beach. After the ceremony, Dylan walked over to me, uptight and jittery. "What's the matter?" I asked. He shook his head in disgust. "I can't believe I didn't shoot today." I was amazed at what I was hearing. "Dylan, it's your wedding day! You can take a day off from basketball." Dylan failed to hear a word I said. While he was in love with Molly, he also had tremendous passion for basketball and the art of shooting. While Dylan's remark may appear too extreme, it truly shows the mindset a top-notch shooter possesses.

YOU GOTTA HAVE HEART!

**"I always believed that if you put in the work, the results will come.
I don't do things half-heartedly.
Because I know if I do, then I can expect half-hearted results."**

Michael Jordan
Future Hall of Fame Player

If you wish to be a great shooter, you must put in a great amount of time. When speaking at youth camps I ask, "Who here would like to be a great shooter?" At this point usually all campers raise their hands. My follow-up question is, "Who here shoots every day?" Only a few hands rise. Finally I ask, "Who shoots once or twice a week?" Normally all hands raise. Call it the innocence of youth or perhaps the age of technology, but I call it the age of naivety.

If a player wishes to receive a college basketball scholarship he must be a "freak." Plain and simple, to get a scholarship, you might be a "freak" of an athlete (in other words, a freak of nature). These are the players who have long arms and legs and a crazy vertical. But most players aren't gifted in these ways. So players that want to receive a basketball scholarship must instead be a "freak" of the gym. These are the players that spend hours upon hours honing their skills, especially in shooting. They don't have the natural talents of an athletic freak, so they must possess learned skills. We call these players "gym rats."

There's an old saying that "a writer writes" and "a painter paints." In basketball, this translates to, "A shooter shoots." I have asked collegiate and professional players that excel in shooting, "What happens if for some reason you can't get out and shoot?" The greatest response is: "Guilt." Dylan had this guilt even on his wedding day. In contrast, poor shooters rarely display guilt when they miss a couple of shooting days. Taking a few days off from the courts just doesn't bother these non-shooting "bricklayers."

Grant Hill, Phoenix Suns veteran, has been quoted, **"What I put into basketball is what I get out of it."** Another saying that is very similar to Hill's quote is: **"Be good to basketball and basketball will be good to you."** One could narrow that down further to: **"Work on the shot and the shot will work for you."**

THE TAO OF SHOOTING

"Basketball is a game of finesse . . .
a coordination of intellect and athleticism,
a harmony of mind and body."
Carl Sagan
Astronomer

One of my players once asked me, "What makes the best shooters so great? Is it that they just practice a lot?" I shook my head and said, "It's more than that. To be a great shooter you must have discipline."

"Discipline? I don't understand," he replied.

So I explained, "Shooting is similar to martial arts. To be a master in karate, you must study karate. To be a master in shooting, you must study shooting. If you want to be the best, you must understand the subject inside and out." I thought back to the top shooters that I've coached and realized that they had a true "Eastern discipline" in their approach to shooting.

I am intrigued at the Eastern culture's discipline, which includes the martial arts and the samurai. The samurai discipline, for example, required endless hours of training and self-denial, while placing an emphasis on spirituality. These activities are based around Taoism. In Taoism, if you wish to be a master of something, then you must perfect not only the technical side of the skill, but the spiritual side as well. In the motion picture, Star Wars, the Jedi was created on Taoism theories. The Star Wars character, Yoda, explained in The Empire Strikes Back, **"A Jedi must have the deepest commitment, the most serious mind."** Of course, the same principle applies to be a "master" shooter.

Becoming a pure shooter begins with a tremendous work ethic and a deep understanding for the art of shooting (and yes, it is an art form). With time, your confidence and "spirituality" will develop and grow. As you continue reading about the mental skills a shooter must posses, you will discover that shooting is not just an act where you throw a ball into a round object. Rather, shooting is truly one of the greatest disciplines in all of sports.

THE DISCIPLINES OF SHOOTING

"I guess you have to be a little crazy to want to spend hours and hours in a gym by yourself."
Kiki Vandeweghe
Former NBA All-Star

Often I ask my shooting students to define the word "discipline." Some shrug, while others give me an answer of, "Something you have to do, but don't really want to do." Today's youngster believes that discipline has a negative connotation. Within the scope of accurate shooting, however, discipline is essential.

My definition of discipline usually differs from the average teenagers' view. In the basketball shooting context, discipline is performing an action or response the correct way and then repeating it again and again in the same manner. Pure jump shooters are some of the most disciplined people in the world. They must do the same shot repetition, often in hostile environments, while playing through fatigue. And through all this, the shooter must always stay relaxed and focused.

Most young players don't understand the true disciplines behind shooting. If you watch a poor shooter, he will release differently on each shot. One release may be to the left, the next may be too high and the third often times will be too low. Great shooters, in contrast, will have the same release point on every shot. If you tell Ray Allen to take ten jump shots and you snap a picture of each of his release points, you will notice his release will be in the same spot each time. In other words, every picture will be identical.

Holding one's follow-through is another example of true discipline. I have yet to see Reggie Miller or Stephan Curry drop their follow-throughs. Every great shooter always holds his follow-through on each and every shot. Reggie would go one step beyond and run down court holding his follow-through (much to the ire of his arch nemesis, Spike Lee).

On the other hand, poor shooters rarely hold their follow-throughs. Many times it appears closer to a high five than a follow-through. Furthermore, an inconsistent shooter often times releases his shot and immediately realizes that his shot has missed as soon as it rotates off his fingers. When this occurs, the player usually pulls his hand away or down rather than holding his follow-through.

I often ask my shooting students if they have seen any great shooter ever pull his hand away after the release. "No," is usually their reply. I then respond, "Why not? After all, it really shouldn't matter that much. That player has already released the ball." But it does matter greatly because not holding your follow-through is an example of how bad habits happen and how shooting slumps occur. Let's say Steve Nash jerks his hand away after the release once out of every ten shots. He becomes so comfortable with it that soon this occurs on every two or three shots. Within a month, Nash's release would jerk on almost every shot. His million dollar shot would soon be worth only a nickel. The bottom-line is that I have never seen an effective shooter that does not hold his follow-through. Once again, it comes back to discipline. If you lack discipline on your jump shot, you probably will not be able to put the ball into the basket with regularity.

DO IT RIGHT...EVERYTIME

"When I was young, I never wanted to leave the court until I got things exactly correct."
Larry Bird
Basketball Hall of Fame Player

Once an individual begins an every day practice routine, discipline must come with it. There's an old saying that "Practice makes perfect." In some ways, this is a flawed statement. The saying should actually be, **"Perfect practice makes perfect."** If you practice with poor habits, your skills will continue to be poor no matter how much time you spend practicing that sport.

An athlete generally develops into the manner in which he practices. If he practices with great effort and discipline, within time his skills will become great. If he practices with average effort and discipline, he will usually only become average. If he practices poorly, he will always have poor skills.

I have never seen a player who practices a great amount of the time, but has virtually no skills. It just doesn't happen. Of course, the same thing can be said for shooting. With proper technique, great discipline, and a great amount of practice time, you will become a great shooter. On the other hand, if you spend limited time on your shot, you will generally have limited shooting abilities.

THE DAWN OF THE THREE POINT LINE

Understanding how to properly train is crucial for total shooting discipline. The three-point shot was first introduced into the NBA in 1979. The college level tinkered with it as early as 1980, but finally adopted it for the 1986-87 season. High school levels followed a year later. Many basketball experts believed the dawn of great shooters would soon happen once the three point shot was firmly in place.

Instead of developing great shooters, however, the three-point line has become a hindrance for accurate shooting at the youth and high school levels. Most of today's young players fail to realize that you must get fundamental shooting skills completely down before you can effectively shoot the three-pointer.

Del Curry is one of the best three point shooters in NBA history. He is also the father of sharpshooter, Stephan Curry of the Golden State Warriors. When Stephan was in elementary school, Del told him he was not allowed to practice three-point shooting until he was in 8th grade. Most young players would rebel at this concept and start shooting three pointers when their father wasn't around. Stephan, however, listened to his father and would not take the "forbidden fruit" of the three-point line. He would develop into a First Team All-American at Davidson and one of the premiere shooters in the NBA (see Del and Stephan's Form to right).

If you see a young player warm-up before a practice begins, you will seldom see him focusing on his form. What you will normally view are players that are "casting" from the three-point line. Because of this lack of discipline, very few players are effective shooters. Most players today are trying to run before they can crawl. To be consistent shooters, players must understand that without shooting discipline, they will always fail.

As mentioned earlier, Europeans are generally considered better shooters than Americans. One of the main reasons behind this is that Europeans do not place emphasis on the three point shot when first learning to shoot. European youngsters are taught shooting techniques at an early age and don't focus on the three point shot until well into their teens. In Europe, the three point shot is not allowed in game competition until age 13. Because of these rules, young players throughout Europe develop better form and focus on their shooting techniques than American youngsters.

Bill Bayno, scout for the Portland Trailblazers and former head coach at UNLV, has been overseas numerous times scouting players. He believes that the three point shot in America acts as "poison" to younger players. "In short, these youngsters fall in love with the line and therefore forget to focus on their form." Bayno believes if the United States adopted the European's rules, restricting the three point shot in games until age 13, America would see more accurate shooters in the future.

Bayno's idea is 100% correct. In my travels, I see players as young as eight that are trying to make three pointers in practices and games. If we would stick to Del Curry's mindset, our youngsters would be accurate shooters by the time they reached high school.

WARMING UP

As mentioned, poor shooters lack discipline to practice properly, especially when it concerns warming up. Most poor shooters warm-up from the three-point line and beyond. If a coach is running a few minutes late for practice, these players can usually be found shooting wildly from half court.

Disciplined players always warm-up for at least five minutes with one handed shooting or stationary shooting. They understand that a body must be properly warmed up before they can start shooting effectively from long range. Because you are dealing with more fine tuned muscles in the upper body, it generally takes longer to warm-up properly than the lower body region.

"DISCIPLINED GREATNESS"

During the summer of 1996, I worked for the Fila Summer NBA League at Cal State University Long Beach. My job was to secure practice sites for the NBA teams and then make sure they were able to get into each gym location. Once I was there I would stay and watch these practices in their entirety.

Ray Allen was a rookie that year for the Milwaukee Bucks. I had watched Ray a few times on television when he was launching three pointers for University of Connecticut and was eager to see up close why this player was considered to be such a prolific shooter. What I soon discovered is that Ray Allen, despite then being only a rookie, was already one of the most disciplined players in the NBA.

Upon entering the gym, he would take his basketball and go to a basket and shoot stationary one-handed shots. For the first 10 minutes he focused only on his upper body form. It was as if I was looking at an artist creating a flawless masterpiece. Only after he warmed up completely, did he start using his legs. His overall discipline was incredible during his 15 minute warming up phase which included not saying a word to anyone.

CHAPTER 2 WRAP UP:

- To be a shooter, you must put in a great amount of time practicing shooting.
- To be a pure shooter, you must begin with a tremendous work ethic and a deep understanding for the art of shooting.
- Young players must be taught the discipline behind a jump shot.

3. TRUTH AND UNDERSTANDING

"You can't handle the truth."
Jack Nicholson as Col. Nathan Jessup
From the Motion Picture, "A Few Good Men"

Today's youngsters need to know the truth about excelling in sports; the truth that if they don't train and properly practice they will never succeed. Youngsters need to fully understand the commitment it takes to be great and they need to be asked, "Are you willing to work for this?" Next, the coach or parent should add, "Because if you are not willing to, then you shouldn't have the lofty goals that you currently have."

Unfortunately I see many coaches that don't tell their youth and high level players the truth. It is really quite simple: if a player lacks shooting skills, chances are very high that that player will not be very successful. Coaches need to tell their players, "You need to get a more accurate shot" or "You need to get a quicker shot." Very few coaches do this especially at the AAU level because they believe if they say any criticism to a player, he will leave and go to another team.

Coaches don't tell the truth, but often times neither do parents. I have seen countless times parents watch their children cast up brick after brick with poor shooting technique. The response from the parent is usually, "Don't worry about it. Keep trying." The truth needs to be, however, "Start focusing on your shot or you will keep failing." If parents and coaches brought each player into reality, there would me more shooters in this world. It is as if everyone lives in Fantasyland and are afraid to tell the truth.

Players, however, are the biggest liars of all. When new students enter my training classes, I hand them an information sheet that they must fill out without assistance from their parents. At the bottom of the questionnaire are a series of questions that begin with, "What are your future goals for basketball?" Often times the player filling out the questionnaire writes, "To play college basketball." The next question is, "To play college basketball, a player must shoot ___ hours per week." The player usually responds with answers that range from 10-20 hours per week. The last question on this questionnaire is, "I usually shoot ___ hours per week." Of course the answers here are varied, ranging from 2-10 hours.

As I look over these questionnaires, I'm amazed at how naive youngsters can be. The majority of the responses say they want to play basketball after high school, but the answers usually do not coincide with playing at this next level. An example of this is when a player writes down that he wants to play collegiate basketball, that he currently shoots eight hours a week, but he believes it takes 15 hours a week to get to the college level. By this response, the player is saying that he wants something, but is not willing to put in the hours to properly get there.

SETTING YOUR GOALS

"If you don't know where you're going, how will you know when you get there?"
Casey Stengel
Baseball Hall of Fame Coach

When speaking at camps, I always ask the players, "Who here wants to be great?" Of course all hands rise. "Now, how are you going to get there?" I ask next. "Do you have a plan? Do you have well defined goals?" At this point, most of the players look at me similar to a deer in blinding headlights because they simply have not set well defined goals.

Another series of questions on the player's questionnaire is: "Do you believe that you are on the right path to your goals OR do we need to build you a bridge for you to reach these goals?" Usually this is split with half of the players believing that they are on the correct road and the other half believing they need assistance to get where they wish to go (college, professional ranks etc.).

Greatness always begins with a series of well defined and attainable goals. After all, if you don't have a blueprint, how will you know what you actually want to build? It would be like trying to build a house from a pile of lumber, but you lack an overall design. Sooner or later that house will crumble, similar to the player that lacks foresight and a plan.

SHORT TERM AND LONG TERM GOALS

Coaches often preach "team goals", but often fail to ever discuss "individual goals." While basketball is a team game, each player needs to have personal goals that will inspire and motivate him. There are two types of goals a player must constantly employ to remain focused: SHORT TERM GOALS and LONG TERM GOALS.

Short term goals can last from a couple of days to as long as an entire basketball season. These are goals for immediate needs. Short term goals can be for statistics (points per game, rebounds per game, free throw percentage) or can be taking a negative action and forming it into a positive one. An example of this would be if you have a terrible shooting release and you give yourself a short term goal of training one week to correct it.

Recently, I have begun using short term goals more with my shooters. When a player is not shooting a certain way because he is being uncoachable or is unfocused, I will tell him, "I'm getting old and I'm starting to lack patience the older I get. When are you going to get this concept down? I need a day. Pick one." We will then agree on a day that his form will change from a negative aspect to a positive one. Every time I see that player I will remind him that day is approaching and ask him,

"Are you working on that change?" Short term goals are very important in building a pure and accurate shot.

A long term goals is intended for players seeking an enduring commitment in basketball. These goals can last from a year to an entire college and professional career. Long term goals can focus on certain basketball aspects. A perfect example of this would be a player setting two years aside to become a great shooter. Long term goals also include the level of play you wish to one day achieve at (high school varsity, college, and or professional).

DO IT RIGHT—ALWAYS

"If you see a guy with good form,
nine out of ten times he can develop into a good shooter."
Ron Boone
Former ABA All-Star

When I first work with a player I ask him to take a series of ten shots. I estimate that 50% of these first time students have no concept of what they are doing when they are shooting. The releases are all over the place and often times these players fail to hold their follow-throughs.

"Can I ask you a question?" I often ask my new student.

"Sure," is the usual reply.

"Do you watch the NBA?"

"Yeah," the player usually replies.

"Have you ever seen Kobe shoot?" He will usually nod. "Does he shoot like this?" At that point I will mimic that player's out of control shot.

"No."

"What about Carmelo Anthony or Ray Allen? Have you ever seen either of them shoot like this?" Once again I imitate that player's shooting form. "But YOU shoot like that," I respond. "In other words, no pure shooter in the NBA or college shoots like you. RIGHT? You better either change your shot OR keep your shot and MAYBE you just might revolutionize shooting. A word of advice—it's easier to change your shot than revolutionize the entire sport of basketball." When the player is faced with those options, he suddenly becomes much more coachable and open-minded.

"YOUR WAY LEADS TO THE HIGHWAY"

From 2001-2003 I coached Zach Luther from my Orange County youth traveling team, "Shooting Stars." Zach played for the "Stars" for two seasons. During this time I would often talk sports to Zach's father, Ed. Ed Luther played five seasons (1980-85) as a backup quarterback for the San Diego Chargers. During this time the San Diego Chargers were one of the greatest offensive football teams to ever step on a field. They were led by NFL Hall of Fame quarterback Dan Fouts and perhaps the greatest group of receivers to ever play the game. They included: Hall of Fame tight end Kellen Winslow and wide receiver Charlie Joiner (who at that time played in more games than any receiver in the history of the league). Wes Chandler and John Jefferson also were both four time Pro Bowl selections. If you think back to the greatest offensive machine in any sport, San Diego's "Air Coryell" would be at the top of the list.

One day Ed and I were talking about his Charger playing days. "You know what was really amazing is that our receivers were not the fastest, nor the best athletes. But they always understood what the coaches wanted. After awhile it became a running joke."

Ed Luther explained that every training camp the Chargers brought in rookie and free agent receivers with as much or more athleticism as the receivers they currently had. Each training camp they lined up in a receiver's line and the coach would tell the group what pattern to run. For example, the coach would tell the receivers, "We're going to run a slant to the corner." The receivers would then run the pattern one at a time. Wes Chandler would start the line and run a flawless pattern. Charlie Joiner would be next and would run the same flawless slant. Kellen Winslow would copy the route once again in a perfect manner. Then the rookies and free agents would follow. "Billy Bob" from "Texas Eastern" would improvise and run the slant the way he wanted to run it. The next rookie would also makeup his own pattern and the player after him would do the same.

"If they would have just watched the Hall of Fame players in front of them and noticed how they ran the route, and then copied the same thing, those players might have made the team. But they never did because they always wanted to do it their way," Ed explained to me.

Accurate shooting is very similar to Ed Luther's story. Kobe Bryant, Deron Williams and Jimmer Fredette have picture perfect shots. Unfortunately, today's players and coaches rarely STUDY the game, let alone understand what a proper jump shot looks like. They may watch a game, but too often don't FOCUS on jump shooting. Most of the time the brain and eyes are only paying attention to the next dunk. If players and coaches would try to duplicate the shooting form of a pure shooter, they would discover their overall shooting would drastically improve.

CHAPTER 3 WRAP UP:

- Today's youngsters need to know the truth about excelling in sports.
- Greatness always begins with a series of well defined and attainable goals
- There are two types of goals a player must constantly employ to remain focused: short term goals and long term goals.
- Short term goals usually last from a couple of days to as long as an entire basketball season. These goals are for immediate needs.
- A long term goal is designed for players who are seeking an enduring commitment in the sport of basketball.

4. UNDERSTANDING FAILURE

**"You're not always going to be successful,
but if you're afraid to fail, you don't deserve to be successful."**
Charles Barkley
Basketball Hall of Fame Player

For many of my students, failure is the hardest aspect to comprehend when learning new shooting techniques. No individual ever wants to fail at anything he does. I have yet to meet a player that proclaims, "I want to be a poor shooter." I have also never met anyone who remarks, "I really don't care if the ball goes in."

President Theodore Roosevelt, once wrote, **"He who makes no mistakes makes no progress."** And of course shooting is really no different. Players need to realize that no one ever succeeds at first. In fact, there will be more failures than successes when learning a new skill. With shooting there will always at first be more misses than swishes. When you understand that there is no such thing as instant success, you should relax as you will no longer be preoccupied by the outcome of the shot.

In a way we were much smarter when we were two years old than we are today. When we were first trying to walk we would fall down (which in a way is the ultimate failure). We didn't lie down and feel sorry for ourselves, however. On the contrary, we would get right back up and try it again. When we were that age, failure never entered into our mindset. It's only after people tell us what we can't do something, that we actually start thinking about being defeated.

As we get older and think about failure as being uncomfortable, we are hit with a double whammy. We often make our life decisions based upon pleasure and pain. Because many of the players that I train have had the same shot for a decade, change can become difficult for them to comprehend. Many times players talk themselves into believing that discomfort (even though it is only for a moment) is a terrible condition.

FAILING 5 MINUTES FOR A LIFETIME OF SUCCESS

**"Our greatest glory is not in never failing,
but in rising every time we fail."**
Ralph Waldo Emerson
American Author, Poet and Philosopher

Players in elementary school understand discomfort much better than high school athletes. Younger players are much more receptive to change and also believing in the teacher. High school players, on the other hand, make their decisions based on how it feels and how they believe the shot appears.

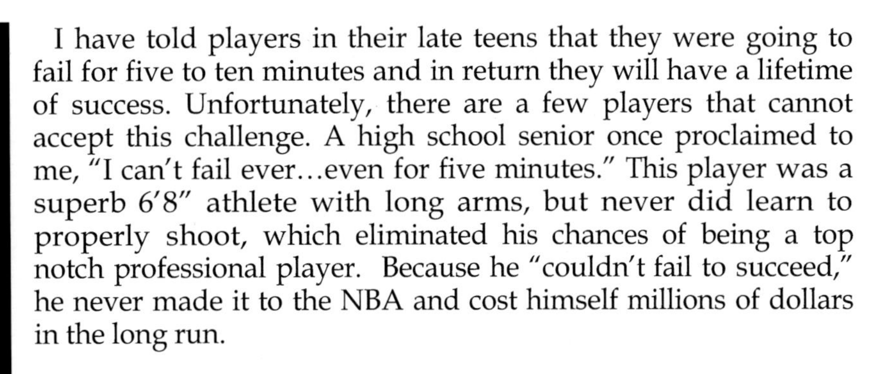

I have told players in their late teens that they were going to fail for five to ten minutes and in return they will have a lifetime of success. Unfortunately, there are a few players that cannot accept this challenge. A high school senior once proclaimed to me, "I can't fail ever…even for five minutes." This player was a superb 6'8" athlete with long arms, but never did learn to properly shoot, which eliminated his chances of being a top notch professional player. Because he "couldn't fail to succeed," he never made it to the NBA and cost himself millions of dollars in the long run.

When learning a new shot, you must look at it similar to a strange science experiment. You need to realize that you will fail, but this will only be short-term failing. You must constantly remind yourself that the positives concerning change will outweigh the negatives. I can generally see which players will ultimately fail and those that will succeed on the hardwood by how they deal with failure. Often I see players get so emotionally upset by a series of short misses that I swear they are ready to have a breakdown on the court. I've also had some parents whose hopes ride on every shot that their child attempts. When their child misses a few shots, the parent starts moaning and becomes more tense which forces the child to also become anxious.

In shooting you can't ever stop what you're doing simply because you're failing. You must continue to move forward. Imagine if you're playing the piano and every time you make a mistake, you stop playing and walk away. You would never improve as you would always be stuck on the first bars of the practice song. Shooting is really no different. You can never be afraid to fail or get upset when you fail. Instead, take a deep breath and refocus your mind. Moving in closer for a few shots probably wouldn't hurt either.

EVERYONE FAILS AT SOME POINT

Everyone has bad shooting sessions, practices and games. John Starks, the former sharpshooter from the New York Knicks, shot a dismal 2-18 in Game 7 of the 1994 NBA Finals against the Houston Rockets.

Kobe Bryant also has had nights where he could not find the rim. In the 2004 Finals against the Detroit Pistons, Kobe clanked, rattled and rolled the ball off the rim. In the last three games of the Finals, Kobe shot 19-59 from the field as the Lakers went down to defeat each time.

Michael Jordan has had his moments of appearing very much like a mortal man as well. In his 1997 Nike commercial, Jordan remarks, **"I've missed more than 9,000 shots in my career. I've lost almost 300 games. Twenty-six times, I've been trusted to take the game winning shot and missed. I've failed over and over and over again in my life. And that is why I succeed."**

"EARLY MORNING MISSES"

In July, 1990, I invited Jeff Fryer to speak to the Marina High School boys' basketball program (located in Huntington Beach, California). Fryer was a great shooter from nearby Loyola Marymount University. He had just helped the Lions to the NCAA Elite Eight. In the process they would shatter many NCAA team scoring marks as well. Loyola was an offensive juggernaut and Jeff was the long distance shooter that rained threes for the Lion's attack.

Jeff came into the Marina gym looking a little disheveled. After all, besides being a terrific shooter, Jeff was also known as a beach "dude" from nearby Corona del Mar. I introduced Jeff as one of the greatest shooters in NCAA history. I don't believe I was stretching the truth one bit. He still holds the NCAA playoff record for most three pointers made in a game with 11 (against the defending NCAA Champions, Michigan) and is fourth all time with 27 makes in an NCAA playoff tournament.

The players at Marina were excited to see how well Jeff Fryer could shoot. It was 9 am and much to my dismay, we quickly discovered that Jeff's jump shot does not actually come out to breathe until well past noon. On this day the three-point king couldn't get the ball into the basket. I learned a valuable lesson that day—every shooter can fail; even if he is considered to be the best.

THE LONG SHOOTING MARATHON

Through my years of shooting instruction, I have discovered that it generally takes two years of discipline, change, failure, and practice to become a great game shooter. This is a very long commitment for most players. I once told a player that it takes two years to develop great skills to which he responded, "But I want to be Michael Jordan right now." Unfortunately it doesn't work that way.

Please understand that you may not see tremendous improvement the first week in your shooting percentage. What you should look for is the difference in distance that you used to miss with your old form and how far you are missing with your new form. Often, I will meet a player for the first time and notice that his average miss is 4-6 inches. Two weeks later the average miss will be only by two inches and within a month that player will be making the shots that he was missing only days before.

WHERE'S THE TEACHER?

"I can only show you the door.
You're the one that has to walk through it."
Laurence Fishburne as Morpheus
From the Motion Picture, "The Matrix"

Buddha once wrote, **"When the student is ready, the teacher will appear."** This is one of the best quotes I have ever come across, and definitely one of the most revealing concerning shooting. As a shooting instructor, I am only as good as the student that I'm instructing. If the student wishes to listen and has an eagerness to improve, I can take him as far as he wishes to go in shooting. If the player can't accept change and failure and completely ignores instruction, there is little chance he will ever improve. You must always want to be taught for learning to occur.

"BUDDHA MEETS BRIAN"

In 1999 I received a phone call from Dinos Trigonis, the director of the Fullcourt Press Scouting Service. Dinos asked me if I would take a look at a young point guard, Brian Baker, who was on his traveling team. Brian was a high school freshman from Mater Dei with excellent ballhandling skills but was a below average shooter. I gave him a one-hour lesson, but it was obvious that Brian was there simply because his dad and Dinos wanted him to be there. He didn't seem very interested in changing his form.

I didn't hear from Brian Baker for over four years. During that time he helped lead Mater Dei to a California sectional title and then received a scholarship to Central Missouri University, a Division II school. Out of the blue one June afternoon Brian called me. "Coach, I need your help."

"Brian, I tried to helping you four years ago. Why is this time going to be different?"

"Before I left for the summer I had a meeting with my college coach and he told me that if I don't get a jump shot my scholarship will be revoked. I have to learn how to shoot this time." It was amazing how receptive Brian suddenly was to failure and change now that his athletic future was in doubt.

KEEPING THE MIND OPEN AND LISTENING

"Gump! Why did you put that weapon together so quickly, Gump?"
Drill Sergeant
"You told me to, Drill Sergeant."
Tom Hanks as Forrest Gump

"HARDWOOD INNOCENCE"

Author and longtime entertainer Art Linkletter has been known to say, "Kids Say the Darndest Things." Sometimes what comes out of a child's mouth is so innocent that it actually makes perfect sense. In October 2003 I was conducting my basketball academy at Soka University (located in Southern Orange County). That night I was focusing on the shooting release, but quite a few of the students were resisting the finger method (a shooting technique we will discuss later). I brought everyone together and mentioned that nine-year-old Jeremy Bass was the only player correctly using the finger on his release.

"Jeremy, you're the best shooter out here and you have the best technique. Why do you use the finger?"

Jeremy looked at me confused and then innocently smiled, "Because you told me to." While I was looking for an answer closer to "because the finger makes the shot stay straight," it was still a thought provoking reply.

"Exactly right," I replied. "And if everyone here did exactly what you just said, each player would be able to shoot the ball correctly."

Forrest Gump is a fictional character and Jeremy Bass was an innocent nine year old when he uttered the above comment, and yet, they both fully understood the concept of being coachable and not trying to resist instruction. If you will just listen, learn and believe, you can go as far as you want in shooting.

"I DO WHAT I'M SUPPOSED TO DO"

What made Michael Jordan so great was not only his athleticism and his competitive spirit, but his willingness to be coached.

Former University of North Carolina head coach, Dean Smith witnessed Jordan's coachable attitude the second day of practice his freshman year. "I was teaching some pressure defense principles and saw Michael was doing it incorrectly," Smith commented. "I went over it with him. I thought it would take him two weeks to learn it.

The next day, Michael had it down perfectly. I said, 'What did you do, stay up all night studying?'

He said, 'Coach, I am a good listener. I do what I'm supposed to do.'"

Jordan never resisted his coaches from grade school to his last season with the Washington Wizards. One day I was speaking with former Chicago Bulls strength and conditioning coach, Chip Schaeffer, and asked him, "How easy was it to train Jordan? Coach Schaeffer smiled and said, "Easy. One thing about Michael is that he always held all of his coaches with the highest reverence."

CHAPTER 4 WRAP UP:

- People don't want to fail in anything they do.
- Players have to realize that no one ever succeeds at first.
- With shooting, there will be at first more misses than swishes.
- Failure will always occur when trying something new.
- We make our decisions in life based upon pleasure and pain.
- You will fail five to ten minutes for a lifetime of success.
- You cannot be afraid to fail or get upset when you fail.

5. WHAT DOES THE PLAYER WANT?

"What the mind can conceive and believe, it can achieve."
Napoleon Hill
Founder of the Science of Success

If you don't believe shooting is important for overall success, chances are excellent that you will never become an accurate shooter. Remember back to the story of the player who failed to realize the importance of shooting, which ultimately cost his team a league championship.

It really comes down to which players possess "shooting maturity." I have coached players as young as ten years old that understood the significance of shooting and comprehended that if they wished to become a top notch player, they had to become an efficient shooter. I have also "attempted" to coach high school juniors and seniors and college players that were not interested in becoming a quality shooter and therefore tuned out my instruction completely. With time, a player can develop this shooting maturity. For some players it can take weeks, others will take months or even years before they understand the importance of being an effective shooter.

"BECAUSE I WANT TO GET IT."

One afternoon in 2001 I had a group of students in my shooting academy that were failing to understand the concepts of holding their follow-through and having shot discipline. That afternoon, only seventh grader, Lauren Sims, truly understood the importance of having proper shooting technique. She was the only player holding her follow-through every time and focusing on each shot. Of course, she was also the only player consistently making her shots. Finally, I stopped and turned to Lauren. "Why is it that you are the only one here that truly understands? Why do you get it?" Surprisingly, I caught Lauren off guard that day because she didn't know how to respond. The next morning I received an e mail from Lauren that read:

Dear Coach Hoover,

Remember how you asked me yesterday, "Why do you get it?" I didn't know how to respond. After thinking about that question all night I finally have an answer. ***BECAUSE I WANT TO GET IT.***

Thanks,
Lauren Sims

Lauren had great shooting maturity and understood the discipline and dedication that it took to become a great shooter. Lauren truly got it! Five years later she would sign a scholarship to Long Beach State University.

"WHY ARE YOU HERE?"

When I was 13 years old my mother bought me a guitar and arranged for me to begin a series of guitar lessons. I really didn't want to play the guitar. Instead, I wanted to go outside and shoot baskets. Finally, I agreed to take guitar lessons for one month.

The first day the instructor taught me some basic cords and then told me, "Go home and practice an hour a day. I'll see you again at this time next week." I went home, put the guitar down and picked up a basketball. I returned to the guitar lesson a week later without having practiced. The instructor started over from the basics because I had failed to learn my cords. He once again told me to go home and practice. The next week I returned having practiced my basketball skills, but not my guitar cords. Finally the guitar teacher asked, "Why are you here?"

When I work with many athletes, I often ask the same question that my guitar instructor posed to me over 25 years ago. Obviously if you don't practice your shooting skills, you will never be able to shoot. It becomes more than just going out and shooting. You must understand what you are doing when you shoot which includes focusing on not just your physical abilities, but also using your mental skills. Most important, you must want to become a good shooter and thoroughly understand the significance of accurate shooting. If this is not significant to you, then you will never become an accurate shooter.

GOOD TEACHER, BAD STUDENT

"We should not have to push you to work hard.
You should work hard because you want to be a great player."
Bob Knight
Basketball Hall of Fame Coach

Dee Wilhite was one of the best teachers that I ever had. Mrs. Wilhite was my senior English teacher at Los Amigos High School (Fountain Valley, California). She was a demanding and stern educator who made you either get serious about the subject or else drop her class. I learned a great deal from her concerning discipline and putting forth my finest effort. Upon finding out in early September that she was going to be my teacher for the upcoming fall semester, I accepted this as a great challenge. Other students in the class moaned and took the defeatist approach by griping, "There's no way I'm going to pass her class." And of course they didn't pass. She failed 40% of the students because they didn't approach her class in a challenging manner. Similarly, if you wish to become a great shooter, you must approach shooting in the same manner that I approached Mrs. Wilhite's class. You must accept the challenge.

If Mrs. Wilhite was such a terrific teacher, then why were so many students failing her class? If you're a great teacher, shouldn't all your students be passing? Of course not. While there are good teachers, there are also bad students. These are students that don't find the subject matter interesting or they are generally apathetic. When it came to playing the guitar, I was a terrible student because I failed to practice. Playing the guitar did not interest me and therefore I was unmotivated and not improving.

During the 1994/95 school year I taught freshmen English at Muir High School in Pasadena, California. Because I'm passionate about writing, I had an unlimited extra credit policy. The students in my classes could write on any subject matter and I'd give extra credit. It didn't matter what they wrote as long as each student was writing. There was only one problem with this concept. Half of the students in my class never took me up on this extra credit proposal and never raised their grade. In fact, over 50% of the class received a D or an F for their final grade. In the long run, I realized that there are some students you just can't motivate because they don't want to be motivated.

"THE IDIOT BECOMES A GENIUS"

At one time I believed Ed Palubinskas did not know what he was doing. Coach Ed was Shaquille O'Neal's shooting coach who received limited results at the free throw line from the "Great Aristotle." I would watch the television in disgust every time Shaq stepped to the charity stripe. More than once I uttered, "Just give me ten minutes with Shaq and I'll change his life forever." I probably wasn't the only coach in the world who has said those exact words. As I watched Shaq miss time after time, I started believing this Australian coach was stealing Shaq's money.

Then I met Coach Ed and my opinion drastically changed. We sat down and spoke in great lengths about shooting one Saturday afternoon. He gave me new shooting concepts that would help my students. We also talked about Shaq and his troubles at the line. Coach Ed remarked, "Shaq doesn't want to be a great free throw shooter. He just wants to be average." Of course, those individuals who wish to be average in anything usually turn out to be below average, which is exactly where Shaq was when it related to free throw shooting.

There are coaches who still believe (as I once did) that Coach Ed didn't know what he was doing concerning teaching shooting because of the Shaq experience. I feel very fortunate to have met Coach Ed and in the process I learned a valuable lesson about not judging people until I know all the facts.

TRUST THE TEACHER

**"We make sacred pact. I promise teach karate to you,
you promise learn. I say, you do, no questions."**
Pat Morita as Mr. Miyagi
From the Motion Picture, "The Karate Kid"

To become a successful shooter you may need to forget what you have learned in the past when it concerns shooting. You may have learned some different shooting aspects, but you must trust that everything in the Pro Shot System makes perfect sense and has a reason behind every action.

The most common ways to teach shooting today are derived from concepts well over 50 years old. Basketball is an ever evolving sport. The game is currently played with a different style and speed than it was 25 years ago. While certain aspects in basketball never change (the give and go and the pick and roll), shooting is always evolving because players are quicker, taller, and better athletes than even a decade ago. Just because a player could get his shot off in the 60's does not mean he could get that same shot off in today's fast-paced game. While most current coaches understand the importance of shooting, it continues to be the most misunderstood and poorly taught skill in all of sports because many coaches have failed to keep up with the changes.

When speaking at camps, the first thing I do is to have everyone seated at the three-point line. Then, I bring a camper up for demonstration purposes. "I know many of you have been taught how to shoot by your past coaches. Today we will take this player here and mold him into what a shooter should look like by what you have been taught." The campers will shout out important aspects of what they believe a shot looks like. The most common responses are:

- "Bend your knees."
- "Start the ball over your head."
- "Keep your back straight."
- "Square your feet to the basket."
- "Get your feet wide."

We then transform the camper to look like the picture on the left. "Let me ask everyone a question— does this person look like he's comfortable?" Sometimes I'll even ask the camper if he is comfortable. "And this is how your coaches want you to shoot? Being uncomfortable and tense? One more question— who shoots like this in the NBA or WNBA?" There is always an eerie silence that follows. "Then why should we ever shoot in this manner?"

CHAPTER 5 WRAP UP:

- A shooter must keep an open mind, not be afraid to fail, be disciplined and practice everyday the correct way.
- If you wish to become a great shooter, you have to be coachable and put forth many hours of practicing and honing your shooting skills.
- While there are good teachers, there are also bad students.
- There are some students you just can't motivate because they don't want to be motivated.
- To become a successful shooter you may need to forget what you have learned in the past when it concerns shooting.

6. BELIEVING

"Come on, fellows. Rome wasn't built in a day."
Coach Buttermaker
"Yeah. It took several hundred years."
Oglivie
From the Motion Picture, "The Bad News Bears"

Many players expect success to occur instantly. These impatient athletes rarely want to wait and expect perfect shooting will take place over night. Many times they will see the extraordinary shooting of Ray Allen or Dirk Nowitski and figure they can do the same.

As mentioned earlier, it is important to remind young athletes excellence in anything takes time. In other words, **"Shooting is a marathon, not a sprint."** You will have many basketball moments that will feature huge up sand massive downs. The same thing can be said concerning your jump shot. Understand, if you lack patience and discipline, you will usually lack an overall accurate shot.

"FROM THE WORST TO THE BEST"

In February of 1998 Glen Oliver called me from Crestline, located in the mountains of Southern California. Glen informed me that his eighth grade son, Kurt, and he would travel down the mountain and check out one of our Sunday shooting sessions. Because our location was two hours away from Crestline, I did not expect Glen and Kurt to show. To my surprise, the Olivers were right on time. Quickly, I noticed Kurt had a slow and stiff shot. "Where did you get that shot from?" I asked.

That's what I've been taught by my coaches."

"Listen, if you want to become a good shooter, you need to believe everything I will teach you." And that's exactly what Kurt did. During the next five years, Kurt would train with me 3-5 times a month. Because he was so receptive and open-minded, Kurt improved and developed into my shooting poster child.

Each year Kurt greatly improved his shooting accuracy and overall speed. He successfully made 35 three pointers on his freshmen team. On varsity he would then make 55 threes as a sophomore, 85 threes as a junior and finally 113 as a senior. The 113 makes would be the leading three-point mark in eight connecting western states. For his abilities and hard work, Kurt received a full scholarship to Pacific Lutheran in Spokane, Washington. The Kurt Oliver shooting story is very special one as it clearly depicts that a young player with a terrible shot can improve to the point where he can go on to break records.

NEVER STOP BELIEVING AND ACHIEVING

"One minute you can be a McDonald's All-American and the next minute you can be working at McDonalds. You have to always make sure you are getting better."
Jason Wright
Basketball Trainer

When a player becomes satisfied with his overall skill level, he disappears quickly from the basketball radar screen. Great players work diligently to improve their weaknesses. They are never satisfied no matter how good they become. Karl Malone was a terrible free throw shooter in his first NBA season, but in time he would break free throw shooting records. After leaving the University of North Carolina, Michael Jordan's greatest weaknesses were defense and shooting. He would over time make those his strongest traits. Magic Johnson was considered only an average shooter when he entered the NBA. With time, he led the league in free-throw percentage.

A basketball player should never rest on past accomplishments. A great player looks at himself as a sculpture that may never be fully completed. This individual is always improving because his skills are always escalating. Walt Disney understood this principle and he believed that nothing worthwhile should ever be completed. Disney once commented, **"Disneyland will never be completed. It will continue to grow as long as there is imagination left in the world."** He realized that anything great must be a continual work in progress.

"YOU CAN TEACH AN OLD DOG"

Kari Johnson, the assistant athletic director at UC Irvine and a former player of mine, called me in the spring of 2000 and asked if I had any jobs for a player in the Anteaters Basketball program, Sean Jackson. At that time, I needed an assistant shooting coach so I agreed to meet with Sean. A 6'5" junior swingman, Sean was very articulate and candid. "I don't know much about shooting. I'm more of a slasher," he uttered. Needing a coach desperately, I didn't have time to shop around. I was just hoping Sean would learn quickly on the job.

Sean was a very fast study. He implemented the shooting methods that I was teaching in his own shot. Before he began working for me, Sean was an average 3-point shooter (shot 32% his junior campaign for UC Irvine). A few months later, with the new techniques and additional knowledge, Sean would shoot 49% from the three-point line making him the #2 three-point shooter in all of NCAA Division I Men's Basketball. Against UC Santa Barbara on national television (ESPN) Sean made five three pointers by halftime. The ESPN announcers played back first half game footage of Sean shooting and remarked, "This is how you shoot a basketball." Due to his efforts of successfully changing his shot, Sean has played professionally in Germany.

Often it can be near impossible to find a mature player to be as receptive as Sean. Many high school, collegiate and professional players believe in the old adage of "You can't teach old dog new tricks." Sean explaining he was not considered a good shooter is a rare disclosure for a collegiate player to make. Sean then later changing certain aspects of his shot is even a rarer feat. I don't believe in that saying at all. As long as the student is receptive and wishes to learn, he can greatly change if he keeps his mind open.

WHY CAN'T DARIUS SHOOT?

Each year I come across many tremendous athletes lacking shooting skills. I wonder to myself—why can't these players become disciplined enough to shoot effectively?

Darius Miles was one of the best athletes in the NBA. In 2000 he entered the league straight out of high school and at 6'9" was believed by many basketball experts to be the next Kobe Bryant. There is only one problem, however. Darius Miles was a very poor shooter. His career three point field goal percentage was 12% and his free throw percentage was 59%. This "can't miss" athlete became an ineffective journeyman his whole career. If Darius would have been an effective shooter he would have been one of the best players in the NBA. His point total would have doubled while he would have been near all-star selection.

There are numerous players like Darius Miles currently playing professionally, collegiately, and at the high school level. These players possess athletic talent, but lack much needed shooting abilities. A few of these athletes will be able to play collegiately because they are such "freaks" of nature. However, they will never get the most they can out of their careers without becoming effective shooters. If you look at the top 20 scorers in the NBA and you take Dwight Howard out of the equation, the good majority of them are excellent shooters especially from the foul line and in the mid-range area (15-20 feet). These include: Kobe Bryant, Kevin Durant, Carmelo Anthony, Paul Pierce, and Dirk Nowitski.

It is alarming to see how many great athletes ignore the importance of accurate shooting. What's even more incredible is the number of younger players who have closed their minds about developing shooting skills and techniques.

SHOOT THE ROCK AND BELIEVE

"You will always miss 100% of the shots you don't take."
Wayne Gretzky
NHL Hall of Fame Player

You cannot score points if you don't shoot during a game. If you're afraid or hesitant to shoot, you will rarely have the opportunities to get your shot off. Dennis Scott, the NBA's all-time three point leader for one season, was asked, "What does it take to be a great shooter?" Scott responded, **"The biggest thing, you've got to have is a big heart and you've got to have confidence."**

Former Loyola Marymount sharpshooter, Jeff Fryer had a very simple approach to shooting in a game. Fryer's effective motto was, **"Shoot until you miss, miss until you make. In other words, always shoot the ball."**

An important rule that I have with each team I coach is, **"If you don't shoot and you're open, you will come out."** A player cannot prosper if he has shackles on his hands and feet during a game. Giving a player freedom to shoot can pay huge dividends in the long run for that individual and the team.

WE WILL WIN THIS GAME!

Perhaps the most famous collegiate moment of all time is Christian Laettner's turnaround jump shot from the top of the key to give Duke a 104-103 victory over Kentucky in the 1992 East Regional Championship. It is a play that is played numerous times each year during March Madness. To refresh everyone's memory, Kentucky hits a running shot to take the lead 103-102 and Duke's Coach, Mike Krzyzewski, immediately calls a timeout with 2.1 seconds left.

Cherokee Parks, a Duke freshman that season, explained no Blue Devil player at that moment thought they could win with the exception of Laettner. "We all believed the game was over. Only Christian thought we still had a chance." Throughout the entire timeout Coach K repeated to his stunned team, "We will win this game!" Of course Duke did win with a perfect full court pass from Grant Hill and a perfect shot from the always confident Laettner.

To become a great shooter, you must believe that you will make every shot including the big shot. When you stop believing, you stop achieving. The moment that negativity and doubt enter your mind, you and your shot are in serious trouble.

CHAPTER 6 WRAP UP:

- A great player looks at himself as a sculpture that is never completed.
- A basketball player should never rest on past accomplishments.
- The great players are working to get better and improve on their weaknesses. As long as the student is receptive and wants to learn, he can easily change as long as he keeps an open mind.
- Understand that if you lack patience and discipline, you will generally lack an accurate shot.
- You have to believe. When you stop believing, you are doomed to fail. You cannot score any points if you don't shoot.
- When you stop believing, you stop achieving.

SECTION III:

MENTAL AND PHYSICAL ELEMENTS OF SHOOTING

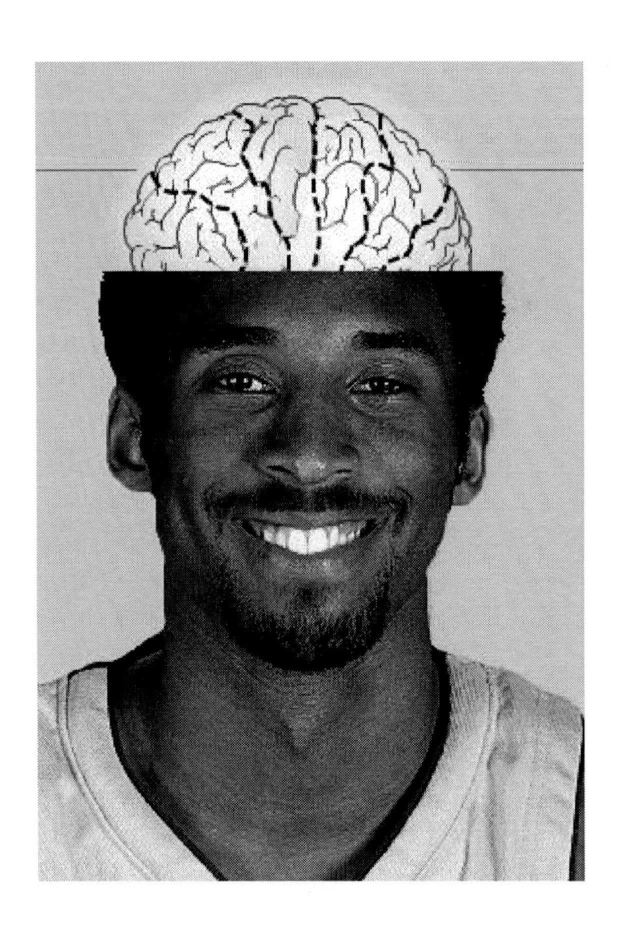

"You be in control of your shot. Don't let your shot be in control of you."

Paul Hoover
Pro Shot Founder

7. MUSCLE MEMORY IMPORTANCE

"Excellence is not an act, but a habit."
Aristotle
Philosopher

Muscle memory is well depicted in the original motion picture, "The Karate Kid."

Daniel LaRusso is a 16-year-old kid who has just moved into a new city and school in Southern California. On the first day of school, he gets battered by a bully who studies karate.

Daniel meets his apartment's handyman, an older Japanese man named Mr. Miyagi. Soon Daniel discovers that Mr. Miyagi is an expert in karate and asks if he will teach him this discipline. Mr. Miyagi agrees, but only after Daniel washes and waxes all of his antique cars. "No problem," Daniel thinks. Mr. Miyagi, however, expects him to put the wax on with one hand in a circular motion and then dry it off with his left hand also in a circular motion. If you have seen the movie you will remember the line, "Wax on. Wax off." Later Daniel also must paint fences and sand the deck in the same disciplined manner.

A few days later, Daniel is tired and angry. He has worked his butt off for Mr. Miyagi, but has been offered little in return. Daniel confronts Miyagi about their original deal to which the old man responds, "I already teach you." Miyagi stands next to Daniel and throws a series of punches at the youngster trying to demonstrate a point. Daniel easily deflects the punches by responding with the same muscle memory that he used when he waxed the cars, painted the fence, and sanded the deck. Miyagi's approach was that you must teach muscle memory first before anything else.

OVER AND OVER AGAIN

"As far as shooting goes, I don't feel pressure in a game.
I've shot so many jumpers in my life, it's just muscle memory."
Casey Jacobsen
College All-American and NBA Veteran

When you become focused and disciplined, you will then repeat the same proper action over and over. After this occurs, you will have obtained muscle memory. The importance of proper muscle memory is critical in basketball, especially when it concerns shooting. Because shooting is an action that uses fine motor movements, muscle memory is crucial. The better the muscle memory in the player, the better the shooter will become.

For undisciplined players, this necessary repetition is difficult (if not impossible) to do. In fact, most players get very bored when they are asked to repetitively practice in order to create muscle memory. Unfortunately for these players, proper muscle memory is what can separate greatness from mediocrity.

It is simply not the act of doing it, but more important it is the act of doing it right every single time. Let's say we go watch NBA All-Star Ray Allen in a shoot-around. When he shoots, his left and right hand will be exactly the same every time. Other parts of his body may change when shooting, but the release and off hand will always remain consistent.

SHOOTING WITHOUT A BALL

When speaking at basketball camps I ask, "Who here shoots without a ball on a daily basis?" Most of the campers look at me as if I just crash-landed my spaceship from Neptune. When I ask most players this question they usually think, "What does shooting without a ball have to do with improving your shot?" Actually, it has everything to do with it. Good shooters shoot all the time without a basketball. They are always trying to improve their muscle memory.

Tim Werdel, Chapman College's all-time leading three point shooter, once remarked to me concerning muscle memory, "I would always shoot without the ball. It became a habit after awhile. I would be at college parties and I'd suddenly find myself shooting without a ball."

Poor shooters never have this much discipline or believe they don't have enough time to work on their shooting without a ball. They usually don't recognize the importance of improving their muscle memory. If you want to be a successful shooter, start taking 200 shots a day without a ball. You will find this does not take a great amount of time and your shooting accuracy will greatly improve over time.

WALKING AND RIDING

"The four laws of learning are explanation, demonstration, imitation and repetition. The goal is to create a correct habit that can be produced instinctively under great pressure. To make sure this goal was achieved, I created eight laws of learning—namely explanation, demonstration, imitation, repetition, repetition, repetition, repetition, and repetition."

John Wooden
Basketball Hall of Fame Player and Coach

Muscle memory is involved when we walk. When an adult walks he doesn't have to think about what he is doing. Because an adult has taken a step so many millions of times, there is virtually no thought process involved. Regular walking is advanced muscle memory requiring no thought process. A baby learning to walk, however, becomes the primary stage of muscle memory. To just take just a routine step at the primary stage, the learner must think of each step as he walks.

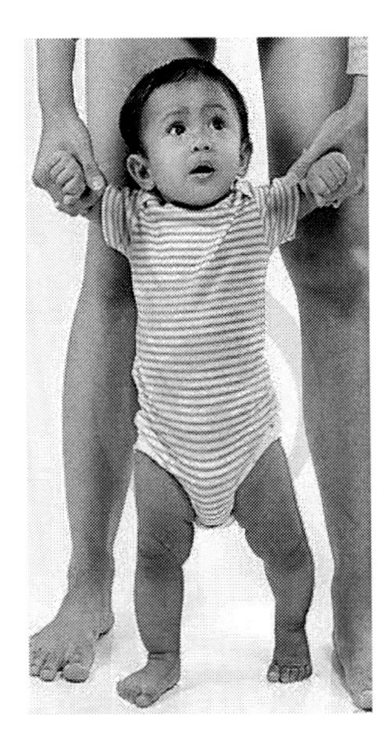

Shooting is similar to learning to walk. At first the shooter must "focus" on his technique. In other words, he must constantly think to perform the action correctly. I have had high school coaches tell me that their players should NEVER think when they shoot, but instead they should have a clear mind. This generally works for advanced and older shooters, but younger players (including most high school athletes) don't have the muscle memory to properly shoot without thinking. Only when the player starts perfecting this technique will he no longer have to think about the action and therefore the shot becomes "automatic."

Muscle memory and shooting are similar to the old notion of riding a bike—"Once you get on, it's like you never got off." If you become a great shooter and have a first-rate shooting touch, you can take many years off and still possess some of this muscle memory. Your shot will not be perfect, but it may be surprising how much memory will still actually be in tact.

"A TRUE MUSCLE MEMORY STORY"

I first began working with Kristen Zoolalian in 1998 when she was in eighth grade. She was a poor shooter with poor muscle memory when I first started training her. Kristen had one thing going for her, however. She was an excellent student who desperately sought to become a great shooter. More than anything, she listened and believed everything I was teaching her. Kristen improved greatly over the next 18 months. She started on the girls' freshmen team at Trabuco Hills High School (Mission Viejo, California).

In late September 2000, Kristen was in her fifth period class when her heart suddenly stopped. She collapsed to the floor and paramedics were immediately called. Nearby teachers gave her CPR and after a few minutes revived her heart. Paramedics rushed her to the nearest hospital where she lay in a coma for two days. After she came out of the coma, Kristen could only mumble a few words and had limited movement in her hands and arms. One day, her mother asked her to do the impossible when they were getting limited results through her body movement. "Kristen, follow-through. Exactly what Coach Hoover taught you." Kristen proceeded to do a follow through motion in her hospital bed.

Kristen had shot so much that she had permanent muscle memory. She could barely move her arms and hands, but still had enough muscle memory to follow-through properly. Kristen returned to the basketball court six months later. Unfortunately, she had enough trauma through the whole ordeal that it was difficult for her motor senses to function properly on a basketball court. She ended up giving up the game she loved so greatly. Kristen did graduate from high school and probably still remembers the many hours that she dedicated to perfecting her shot. When I heard this story from Kristen's mother, Cindy, it was only then that I fully realized the importance of muscle memory and how it can continue with a person well after a player is retired from an activity.

FROM THE BOOK OF MJ

**"You can practice shooting eight hours a day,
but if your technique is wrong,
then all you become is very good at shooting the wrong way."**
Michael Jordan
Future Basketball Hall of Fame Player

Jordan's quote depicts proper and improper use of muscle memory. Simply put, if you practice the wrong way you will receive inadequate muscle memory. A player cannot improve by simply showing up and shooting on a consistent basis.

Proper muscle memory is only achieved through proper practice. Of course, this proper muscle memory is known commonly as "technique." Once you master this you will begin making shots. I have never come across a player who has good shooting form but cannot get the ball in the basket on a regular basis. In other words, shooting is about form and muscle memory.

SURVIVAL TIME

Young players cannot shoot a large number of shots while going as fast as they can for a long period of time because they lack strength and endurance. What happens is that the player begins throwing up shots that no longer resemble proper shooting form. Total exhaustion for a young player hurts his shot much more than it helps.

When it comes to younger players, it is best to focus on proper shooting form rather than running these novice athletes into the ground. I have seen good young shooters hurt their form by focusing not on their shot, but whether they will finish the session in one piece. I call this "survival mode."

Young players and poor-average shooters need to be more concerned about how their shot feels and looks rather than shooting until they drop. If a younger player needs to work on his overall conditioning, he should never do an activity that requires great hand eye coordination and a focused discipline like shooting.

If my young teams or players need conditioning, we will run extra sprints or I will give more time for scrimmaging, but I would never use this for "survival mode" shooting. This training can only assist older and more advanced shooters. Great shooters need to be pushed when it comes to cardio vascular work. For many college and professional players, shooting stamina is crucial.

CHAPTER 7 WRAP UP:

- When you become disciplined and focused, you will start doing the same proper action over and over again. When this occurs, you have just obtained muscle memory.
- The better the shooter, the better the muscle memory.
- Proper muscle memory is what separates greatness from mediocrity.
- A player cannot improve by simply showing up and shooting on a consistent basis.
- Proper muscle memory is only achieved through proper practice.
- When it comes to younger players it is best to focus on proper shooting form rather than running these novice athletes into the ground.
- Young players and poor-average shooters need to be more concerned about how their shot feels and looks rather than shooting until they drop. Other parts of the body can change when shooting, but the release and off hand must remain consistent.

8. SHOOTING IS A LIE!!!

"Shooting is such an amazingly subtle skill."
Peter Brancazio
Brooklyn College physicist

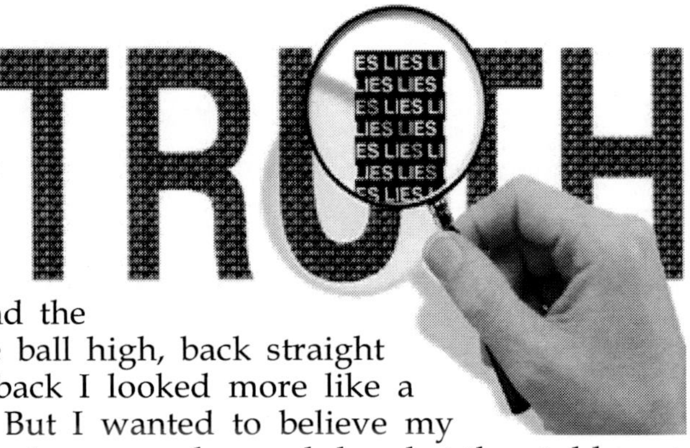

For the past 15 years I have studied the way great shooters shoot and have constantly asked myself, "Why do they shoot differently than how I was taught?"

Growing up in Ventura, California, I was taught by my coaches to: bend the knees, feet shoulder width, start the ball high, back straight and step into your shot. Looking back I looked more like a constipated Elvis than Jerry West. But I wanted to believe my coaches. I was always taught to listen to my coaches and do what they told me to do. What a mistake I would later discover.

When I first started coaching I was an observant sponge. I would watch great shooters for hours AND try to see what they were doing right. Then I would watch my players. Something was missing in the equation. My high school players and NBA sharpshooters were both wearing shorts, sneakers and were from the human species. It was at that point the comparisons stopped. But I believed they just needed a few fine-tuned skills and a little practice and soon they would start shooting like Danny Ainge or Byron Scott.

For many years I called myself a shooting coach and my players were decent shooters, but I wasn't producing the type of pure shooters that I was hoping for. The problem was that I was still haunted by my coaches from the past and those little messages of "square up," "shoulder width" and "bend those knees" continued to linger in my brain.

And then my life changed with a few words from my ex-roommate who was a former Division II head coach. He told me, "You know, no one in the NBA shoots like the way you teach." At first I wanted to tell him to stick it where the sun doesn't shine, but then I did some soul searching and asked myself, "Can he actually be right?" Soon I realized he was correct and a change was definitely needed.

I cleared my head and went back to the drawing board. I studied great shooters in person and by watching endless hours of videotape. I started talking with professional and college coaches regarding shooting. It was then I realized that 90% of what was being taught in most basketball circles was incorrect.

YES—Shooting is a darn right lie and we have fallen for it hook, line and sinker.

No one asks questions of "Why do we do it this way?" Coaches trust their past coaches and players trust their current coaches. The only problem with this "trust" is that this information usually is incorrect.

As I have mentioned many times throughout this book, shooting at the youth and high school levels is like a train wreck: you need to stop and watch, but it is shocking, disturbing and usually makes you lose your appetite. So here's the $1,000.000 question: **WHY CAN'T MOST OF TODAYS PLAYERS SHOOT?**

The answer is very simple: **Players struggle with shooting BECAUSE COACHES ARE TEACHING IT WRONG.**

THE NIGHTMARE CONTINUES

"It's like a nightmare, isn't it?
It just keeps getting worse and worse."
Grady Seasons from "The Color of Money"

Five percent of high school players are good shooters. Another ten percent are average shooters. That leaves 85% of all high school players that are below average to poor shooters.

Imagine if 85% of the Unites States high school students were getting D's and F's on their report cards. This would be the #1 story on the news. It would be on the cover of Time Magazine. Teachers would get fired. There would be lawsuits every where.

So why isn't this happening with shooting? Because we have come to believe shooting is either not important or that a player can't improve his shooting.

DENIAL AND PROCRASTINATION

What bothers me the most is the lazy faire attitude that many coaches have about their team's lack of shooting success. They constantly make jokes about how their player's can't find the basket. You've heard the phrases over the years: "Brick Central," "Brick City," and "Brick House".

There are many coaches that have has come to accept that their teams will always be poor shooters. I live in a college town in Southeast Ohio. I also have a gym in my backyard with three glass backboards and a GUN (an automatic ball return machine). In 2011 I read that the local Division I women's team was statistically the worst shooting team from the three point line. They ranked 344 out of 344.

I called the head coach and explained who I was (my credentials etc) and that her team could train with us anytime at no cost. Her response still shocks me to this day. She replied, "Coach, I'm going to decline your offer. My staff and I have talked and we don't believe our players can improve in their shooting. We have to recruit better shooters. Thanks anyway."

I responded back, "I can't disagree with you more. I always believe ANYONE can improve.

Later I would tell this story to Milwaukee Bucks Assistant Coach, Bill Peterson who responded, "That is pretty disturbing. I can't believe a coach would ever give up on their team like that." Sadly, there are million of coaches that think in this same manner.

Many coaches and players are also known for procrastinating. Many believe the shooting problems that they are suffering will get better ONE DAY. I've heard coaches and players say, "Just give it time." But it never seems to get better. Normally if a player has a terrible shot at the start of the season, they will have a terrible shot at the end of the season. Without a strategic plan, things never get better.

The Pro Shot System needs to be that plan.

PULLEYS AND LEVERS

The Pro Shot System works because it is biomechanically correct.

In the simplest form, the body is a machine of levers and pulleys. Unlike other machines and because of muscle memory, the more you correctly use the body, the better the results become.

The body executing the shot is a machine that must work in unison with five parts of the body. These five parts and their features are:

1) **Shooting Hand and Arm:** Keeps the ball straight.

2) **The Off Hand**: Gives the shot a guide and the body overall balance.

3) **The Elbow**: Supplies the shot with power.

4) **Head and Shoulders:** Allows the shot to be relaxed and tension free.

5) **Lower Body:** Responsible for speed and shooting balance.

Most players never become accurate shooters due to the fact that different parts of the body are working apart and not together. Pure shooters have all muscles, bones and tendons working together to form a tension free and fluid shot.

REASONS FOR MISSING

The Pro Shot System works because it is simple to understand.

A player typically misses a shot for one of three basic reasons: 1) Poor and unfocused release, 2) Lack of power and 3) Tension or pressure.

When speaking of undue tension and pressure, there are subcategories for this that includes: shooting straight up and down, a lack of extension or poor balance. When either of these occur, the body is generally tensing too much. Here are the typical reasons for missing and why they occur:

• **POOR RELEASE**—For younger players, this is the most common reason for missing a shot because they have failed to get the release mechanics down. Having a poor release is usually due to the ball rotating off the wrong fingers or having the follow-through turn to the right or left side. As players advance in their shooting ability and start understanding their release points, undue tension and pressure usually become the troublesome area.

• **LACK OF POWER**—Players can lose their power because they are out of their range or fatigued. For both of these reasons, a shooter must gain additional power developed through the elbow and legs (we call it "sway) as well. Losing power can also be a direct result of undue pressure and tension from the shoulder and neck region. If you tense while shooting, you will generally lose your strength.

• **UNDUE TENSION AND PRESSURE**—Shooters often miss because they feel tension in their shoulders, neck, and the hand regions. Shots that are too long or too short are often due to the player having undue tension and pressure. This reason is the largest cause for missing at the high school varsity, collegiate and professional levels.

- **SHOOTING STRAIGHT UP AND DOWN**—We are taught at a young age to NEVER fade and to shoot in a straight up and down manner. The best shooters in the world, however, don't shoot up and down. Instead they sway their shoulder back which gives less tension while forcing the ball to arc more. If a player is short, 90% of the time the trouble is that they shot straight up and down.

- **LACK OF EXTENSION**—If a player is constantly short, chances are the ball was released too low. Undue tension and pressure will cause a player to have a low release. Being a lazy shooter will also make a player to release below the rim. A shooter must release above the rim at all times.

- **POOR BALANCE**—This occurs when the feet are too wide or narrow, the off hand pulls off the shot uncontrollably, or a player fades to the side. Similar to a diver, balance on a jump shot primarily occurs in two areas—the hands and feet. If either of these regions becomes too wide or too narrow and thus unbalanced, the shooter's accuracy will greatly suffer. By having a poorly balanced shot, the shooter is tense upon the release.

A DELICATE ART

The Pro Shot System works because it is effortless.

An official men's basketball weighs between 20-21.5 ounces; a girl's basketball weighs slightly less. In other words, it's a very light object compared to heavier objects used in other sports (such as a shot-put or a discus). Consequently, shooting a basketball is a nearly effortless activity because the ball is so light and so less energy is needed. The most difficult athletic activity to perform is throwing a shot-put. It takes 680 joules, a metric unit of energy use, to properly throw a shot put. A hockey slap shot requires 170 joules and pitching a baseball requires 120. The act of shooting, however, is the lowest at only 15 joules. Shooting is a fine muscle activity that needs limited power.

Watch a highly muscled football player pick up a ball and attempt to shoot at a basket. He will usually miss long simply because he trains in a sport (football) that focuses on using heavy lifting and large muscles. On the other hand, observe a great shooter and he will always utilize "finer muscles" (including triceps, wrist, fingers and toes). These fine motor skills allow the shooter to be relaxed and make shooting appear effortless.

When a player uses technique wrong, tension develops and the shot suffers. With the Pro Shot System, the shot becomes effortless and the player becomes more accurate and quicker as a shooter.

COACHES AND PARENTS VIEWPOINT

"To change a habit, make a conscious decision,
then act out the new behavior."
Dr. Maxwell Maltz
Founder of Cybernetics

When I evaluate a shooter I will ask the coach or parent, "So what do you think is wrong with the shot?" The two most common responses are either that player "lacks confidence" or "lacks concentration." What the coach or parent fails to understand is that these become the effect, but are not the cause. Obviously, when a player misses shots, he begins losing confidence and will suffer from a lack of concentration.

Poor mechanics (especially in the release hand) is usually the real reason why the ball doesn't go in. It doesn't matter how confident you are as a shooter in the early stages of shooting. If you have poor mechanics, you will generally have a poor shot. When I reflect back to all the great shooters I have seen play at the collegiate level or in the NBA, the majority of these players have picture perfect looking forms. Poor shooters generally have ugly looking forms. In other words, learning good techniques is imperative to becoming an excellent shooter.

With shooting, you either have confidence or you don't. Of course if players had better shooting skills, they would have greater confidence to shoot the ball. Rarely do you come across a great shooter who will not shoot the ball in a game. These players believe that they have trained to become the best and therefore, have the right to shoot the ball in a game.

To be a prolific shooter, proper mechanics is a necessity. A great shooter must train his body to have great shooting form. In other words, he must break his poor shooting habits and replace them with smoother techniques. According to the late Dr. Maxwell Maltz, author of Psycho-cybernetics, **"It generally takes 21 days to form a positive habit."** If you are a true pessimist you can change this belief to: it takes 21 days to break a negative habit. Whatever your belief is, it is crucial to take your bad shooting habits and turn them into positive ones as quickly as possible.

ACQUIRING HABITS

"If an idiot were to tell you the same story every day for a year, you would end by believing it."
Horace Mann
Father of American Education

There are two ways to acquire a bad habit—through a negative influence or a lack of concentration and conditioning over a period of time. A negative influence could be a coach, parent, or a friend who teaches an aspect of shooting the wrong way. While it isn't very comfortable and not easy to perform, you still believe in that instructor. When I see a player whose feet are so wide that he looks as if he's riding a horse, I ask him, "Did someone teach you that?" Nine times out of ten he will say it was his dad or a former coach.

If you are not careful, you can also fall into bad habits over time by lacking focus and discipline. Bill Sharman, from the book, "Sharman on Basketball Shooting, wrote, **"It takes five times more work to break a bad habit than it does to develop a good one."** I've had poor shooters who come to me hoping that I could give them a tiny bit of shooting accuracy. Within time the player developed into a solid shooter, but instead of taking the next step toward improvement, their shot suddenly regressed. Why did this happen? The player has forgotten the disciplines that gave him this first stage of improvement. He received a false sense of confidence and started going away from the techniques that made him improve in the first place.

You will also fail if you do not know what you are doing in an activity like shooting. I'm amazed at the number of young players that attend one of my shooting sessions or camps with little concept concerning accurate shooting. Don't they watch the NBA, WNBA, or college basketball on television? Can't they see the form that Ray Allen, Stephan Curry or Steve Nash possesses? You would think that today's players would pay much closer attention to the best collegiate and professional shooters, but this unfortunately is seldom the case.

Rarely can a player develop into a top-notch shooter without any shooting instruction. After all, how can you become prolific at something you know little about? That would be like trying to fly a 747 successfully without having had any form of training. Chances are that plane would crash and burn every time.

Obviously, the only way to excel at anything is to obtain proper knowledge, become disciplined, and train in that activity. And of course, shooting is really no different. Baseball analyst, Tim McCarver commented, **"Good habits are as easy to form as bad ones."**

The most important objective a player must have is to demolish his poor shooting habits and replace them with positive techniques. This involves both physical and mental activity. As you read along, you will begin to understand how the mental side works in unison with your physical side.

IF IT FEELS GOOD, IT MUST BE GOOD

When attempting to change your shot, there may be some discomfort at first. When adjusting a flawed shot, new techniques may at first lead to awkward movements. Within a week, these movements should become more coordinated, leading to a more comfortable shot.

A shooting coach can often times be an underpaid psychologist. The psyche of most players can be very fragile. It is important that each player understands that there may be some discomfort, but it is also crucial to listen to each player regarding how it feels. Often times, the better the shot feels, the easier the shot becomes.

There are many shooting coaches that believe in the notion of math regarding shooting. This includes knowing the exact degrees of a shot and the study of the arc of the ball. I'm not a math guy. The only thing I know about degrees is at 80 degrees fat people sweat and the arc that I really like is the one out in front of McDonalds.

What I care about, on the other hand, is how the shoot feels to that shooter. During a session, I repeatedly ask the student, "How does it feel?" To properly teach shooting, the coach must be receiving constant feedback.

CHAPTER 8 WRAP UP:

- The body is a machine of levers and pulleys.
- The shot is a machine that must work in unison with five parts of the body. These five parts work properly together by understanding mental concepts, which include focusing, and muscle memory.
- Properly shooting a basketball is an effortless activity because the ball is so light but also because less energy is needed.
- To be a prolific scorer, mechanics are a necessity. It takes 21 days to form a positive habit.
- There are two ways to acquire a bad habit—through a negative influence or a lack of concentration over a period of time.
- If the player is not careful, he can fall into bad habits through time and a lack of overall discipline.
- If you do not know what you are doing in a sport you will naturally fail.

9. THE SYSTEM INTRODUCTION

For 40 plus pages I have explained the importance of shooting, about buying into shooting and understanding change. Now it is time to introduce you to the Pro Shot Shooting System.

Coaches are into acronyms. I use them all the time. Some of my favorite ones are: KISS for Keep It Simple Stupid and KYP for Know Your Personnel.

The most popular acronym out on the market for shooting is BEEF which stands for Balance, Eyes, Elbow and Follow-through. It is what many coaches recite to their players on a daily basis.

In the summer of 2011 we hosted over 200 camps in 40 states. During this time we saw over 1,000 players that subscribed to the BEEF theory. Of those 1,000 players, not one player had a quick and accurate shot. NOT ONE!!!

I truly believe that BEEF does not effectively work. It is a noble idea to simplify shooting concepts, but the error in this lies directly in what it is intended to do. In other words: It's too darn simple.

Balance is important, but what kind of balance? There are some coaches and players that believe if your legs are three feet wide, then this is true balance. Eyes are important because a blind shooter wouldn't make too many shots. But with your eyes, what are you supposed to look at? The ball? The rim? And what part of the rim?

And what about the follow-through? Yes, everyone needs to hold their follow-through. But what should this follow-through look like? What fingers should the ball come off of?

BEEF fails to work because it is not detailed enough. But I still think Acronyms are cool especially when learning a shooting system. So I decided on a long drive from Arizona to Ohio in 2011 to make up something clever that not only works, but is easy to remember.

So as I'm looking at endless Cacti in what seemed to be an endless desert, I started writing down different words. As you will learn very quickly, the Pro Shot System revolves around the "Finger." So I scribbled Finger on my note pad.

Mental focus is everything so the "Aim" was next. In our camps we deal with the lower body and what I like to call the "Rhythmic Hop." Next we always teach the "Turn and finally end up with the "Sway."

So I had my key words down on paper and then I tried to see if there was an acronym that could bring it all together.

- *Finger*
- *Aim*
- *Rythmic Hop*
- *Turn*
- *Sway*

I still believe this is God's best practical joke on me to date. My acronym and Pro Shot's acronym added up to FARTS. **Yes, FARTS!!!**

As I drove on, I thought more about it. Kids love that word and will remember it. And then I realized that not everybody eats BEEF, but everyone…well you get the picture.

We like to say the best shooters are into **FARTS**.

So after long wait, here now is the Pro Shot Shooting System….

:

10. THE FINGER

Proper shooting technique always begins with proper release. I've asked coaches and players, "What's the most important part of a shot?" I get various answers ranging from bending your knees to squaring up to the basket with your feet. Then I add my two cents and explain, "Don't you think the release hand and arm is important? After all, isn't that what you shoot the ball with?" This would be similar to a soccer coach asking players and coaches, "What is the most important element in a kick?" and someone answers, "Your arms." WHAT?

If you watch great shooters, very few of their shots actually miss to the side. The one constant that most pure shooters have is that they always shoot straight. Poor shooters miss in all directions, but often favor missing to the sides. For a poor shooter, missing to the left or right occurs 50% of the time or more. A top-notch shooter, on the other hand, will usually miss to the sides 5% of the time or less.

HOLD THE FOLLOWTHROUGH

Quality shooters hold their follow-through on every shot. The duration a player should hold his follow-through is until the ball hits the rim or net. There are various camps and coaches that instruct players to hold their follow-throughs for three seconds. This becomes too complicated as now you are not only focusing on your shot but also counting in your head at the same time. Holding the follow through until the ball hits the rim or net is much easier for overall focusing purposes.

I've actually heard youth coaches tell their players not to hold their follow-throughs because the shooter must attack the offensive boards for rebounding. These coaches believe that if the shooter holds his follow-through it eliminates all possibilities of ever grabbing an offensive rebound. The logic of this doesn't make sense. While I do believe offensive rebounding is important, you can never waste a shot. I have never seen a quality shooter not hold his follow-through in hopes of grabbing an offensive rebound.

Understand that most players and coaches don't understand the concept of "Follow your shot." Many poor shooters run after their rebound similar to a dog chasing after a ball. I have coached many players who will run after their shot while they are shooting. They get so used to missing that they fail to remember their follow-through and most shooting concepts.

What each player should realize regarding "follow your shot" is that the ball generally bounces the same distance that it is shot. For example, if the ball is shot from the 3 point line, the ball will usually bounce back to the 3 point line. This bounce can be left, right or straight, but probably won't bounce near the basket. When you follow your shot, make sure to always hold your follow-through. Remember—you do not need to rebound your shot if you are always making them. I have yet to see Carmelo Anthony or Kobe Bryant run after their rebound like a dog retrieving their ball.

I have seen thousands upon thousands of players that have completely "broken" shots because they are more worried about "following their shot (which they interpret to "run after the shot") than holding their follow-throughs. Coaches would greatly help their players if the took the "follow your shot" out of their vocabulary forever.

COACH ED AND HIS INDEX FINGER

As mentioned earlier, I met Ed Palubinskas at a Nike Las Vegas coaching clinic in May, 2002. Little did I realize how he would change my entire thinking regarding the shooting release. I sat down with Coach Ed and we chatted for almost two hours on the mental and physical aspects of shooting. I was amazed at how much we were on the same page concerning shooting techniques. Then he dropped a bombshell on me.

"What fingers do you tell your students the ball should come off of?" Coach Ed asked.

"These two." I held up my index and middle finger.

"Why?"

"Well, they are the strongest and they always keep the shot straight." I thought my answer was correctly worded. I was wrong.

"Put your hand straight out." Coach Ed, a strong Australian who reminded me slightly of Nick (Crocodile) Dundee, grabbed my outstretched hand and my index finger. "See, this is the only straight finger you have. These (the other three fingers) mean nothing. Why would you shoot with these? They're crooked. This (the index finger) is what accurate shooting is all about. See—it's perfectly straight. If you use it correctly, you will discover that your shot will always be straight."

I found his index finger theory to be interesting and definitely different from the two finger technique I had taught for years. As he began leaving, Coach Ed gave me a piece of advice. "Try out the one finger. Only a handful of shooting coaches teach it, but they are some of the most respected. It will work. But you have to believe." I agreed to try this new technique and I thanked Coach Ed for his time and advice.

A few days later I returned to Southern California and would tryout Coach Ed's index finger theory first on myself and later on a few friends. While at first it felt awkward, I soon began seeing the logic of using only the "straight" finger. Within a matter of days I was implementing the finger in all my private lessons and clinics. At first, many of these players were hesitant. I would now have each player push down with his index finger harder than before while focusing on that finger. Soon my students shooting percentages rapidly increased. I could also see their overall shooting confidence rising. They started having complete control in their shot's direction. The players that were constantly missing left and right in the past were now suddenly shooting the ball much straighter.

THE INDEX FINGER

The index finger is the finger that truly makes the world go around. It's easily the most important finger on the human hand. When speaking at camps, I ask the campers, "What is the most important finger on your hand?" Then I explain how a person uses the index finger in every day life. "Think about it.

- Your team has just won a championship on a last second shot. You're running around the court like a crazy person. You want to show the crowd that your team is #1. What finger do you hold up? Be careful here. The wrong finger can get you expelled.
- You're mad at your friend. You want to make a point he will remember.
- You get close to them and put your finger in his chest. Which finger will you use?
- A stranger stops and asks for directions to the closest store. You point in the correct direction. What finger do you point with?
- What finger do you dominate your keyboard computer with?"

Of course the answer is always the index finger. It is the strongest finger on the hand and it's also the straightest. It is the finger that when used correctly on a jump shot can determine a player making an all-star team and when it's used incorrectly can get an individual cut from the team. Simply put, the index finger is crucial in life as well as success on the basketball court.

THE GENIUS OF KOBE

In December, 2003 I attended an early season Los Angeles Lakers game. Because a friend gave me tickets to a pair of courtside seats, I went early to watch the Lakers warm-up. Kobe Bryant is an intriguing player. Considered one of the best athletes in the NBA, Kobe has developed into one of the best shooters in NBA history. He currently holds the NBA record (along with Donyell Marshall) for most three pointers made in a game with 12.

While watching the Lakers warm-up, I paid careful attention to Kobe and his release. I discovered Kobe uses a slightly different release than what I was teaching. Instead of pulling the index finger slightly down with the thumb sticking out, he would pinch his shot with the index finger and his thumb. When he did this, the other three fingers would stick up almost like a small group of stairs. In other words, the pinkie sticks up the highest, followed by the ring finger and finally by the middle finger.

Carefully I watched his release and how the ball rolled off his index finger on each shot. Driving home that night I thought about Kobe's release and the shooting discovery that I had just made. Forget the unearthing of King Tut's Tomb, the search for Atlantis or the Fountain of Youth. Those discoveries mean nothing. I had just revealed easily the most important finding—keeping the shot straight. And, I found all this in Kobe Bryant's index finger. In tribute to Mr. Bryant, 18 months later I would name my Black Labrador puppy, Kobe.

Within a few days I showed this technique to all of my students. Most were receptive, but there were some that appeared cautious. For some it took only a matter of moments to fully get the technique down. Others would have to go home and focus for a few days before they understood the technique and felt comfortable using it.

The Kobe pinch made more sense than just having the one finger down for two reasons. The first reason is that it is easier to shoot this way. With the one finger down, the thumb sticks out causing added tension in the hand. There is no tension, however, when using the pinch. When using the Kobe pinch, the shot becomes easier. The second reason to use this technique is that it forces the shot to stay straighter. When you bring the index finger to the thumb, the shot stays straight. When you just use the one finger method with the thumb sticking out, the finger can have a mind of its own. In other words, it can still pull to left or right. This will never happen with the pinch shot. The thumb forces the index finger to stay straight.

"ONE DOWN, THREE UP"

When it comes to shooting instruction, I use a variety of sayings to constantly remind my players of important shooting aspects. One of the most common phrases is, "one down, three up." In other words, the index finger goes down and the other three fingers should remain up. As Coach Ed reminded me, "Why would you shoot with these three fingers?" (middle, ring and pinkie finger). "They're not straight."

The difference between shooting with the correct finger and the wrong fingers is unbelievable when you look at the percentages. After doing research on my students I have developed "the 20% theory." If you shoot the ball off your index finger, you have a 70% chance of making the shot. When it rotates off the index and middle finger together, the player will make it 50% of the time. When it comes off only the middle finger the percentage decreases to only 30%.

Finally, when it is released off the ring finger or the pinkie, the player makes 10% of his shots. In other words, the shooting percentages dramatically decrease 20% with each finger that is used.

THE KEY TO SHOOTING

When you go to bookstores you will see endless books with the words: "The Key." Among them are: "The Key to Life", "The Key to Happiness" and the "Key to a Happy Marriage." Now it's time for "The Key to Shooting". Here it is: **PUT YOUR FINGER ABOVE AND THROUGH THE RIM**. Yes, it's that simple.

When a player moves his finger or arm to the side, he will make it only 1% of the time. That's it!!! Possibly two percent if shooting outside and it's a windy day. When he has his finger through the rim, he will make it 50-80% depending how good of a shooter he is.

I know it sounds too simple, but it really is this simple. I have had professional players mock this and say, "There has to be more to it." Then they try it and they come back and say, "You're right."

The simplicity starts with good shooters miss straight and poor shooters generally miss all over the place, but mostly to the sides. If you want to be a good shooter, shoot straight. If you want to be a poor shooter, continue missing sides. Good shooters miss less than 10% of their shots to the side. Poor shooters may miss as much as 80% of their shoots sideways.

THE SECRET

I truly believe the finger is a secret throughout the basketball world. My belief is that the top players know the finger secret, but tell few about it.

A few years ago one of my students went to Kobe Bryant's Summer Camp. She was very excited to see "the ways of the finger" from the Black Mamba. To much of her surprise, Kobe was teaching the camp the cookie jar method (reach into the cookie jar with all four wingers down). At that point she thought, "That Coach Hoover is a fraud," and "The Pro Shot System is a big fat lie." Still she decided to approach Kobe after the camp ended.

"Kobe, when you shoot, what about the finger?" As she spoke she held up her right hand with the "finger" motion obvious.

Kobe looked at her and smiled and replied, "Oh, you know about the finger." Yes, it really is a secret.

It is interesting that Pau Gasol did not use the finger when he was with the Memphis Grizzlies, but started using it once he got to the Lakers. Strange coincidence or did the secret get passed onto him by Kobe?

DR. EVIL'S FINGER

When speaking at camps and clinics I ask the players, "When it comes to shooting, which finger is your most evil?" Of course most of the players immediately think of their middle finger. "It's actually your pinkie, "I respond back. "I call it your Dr. Evil finger." Of course most of my students know all three Austin Powers movies well and therefore know his archenemy, Dr. Evil. And by knowing Dr. Evil, most of the players also know his mannerisms, which include sticking his pinkie finger out, and putting it next to his mouth. "When you shoot, you definitely don't want to use the Dr. Evil finger. It is evil. It is the worst finger you can shoot off of."

WHO ELSE USES THE FINGER?

"Ninety-eight percent of the shooter's today normally shoot with the index finger."
Pete Maravich
Basketball Hall of Fame Player,
From the Video Series, "Pistol Pete's Homework Basketball"

As I have spread the finger message throughout the world, I have my students on a never-ending mission to discover what famous players are currently using "the finger." The Kobe finger sighting has seen on countless players as: Chauncey Billups, Dwyane Wade, OJ Mayo, Tim Duncan, Diana Taurasi, and Maya Moore. Yao Ming, Grant Hill, Allen Iverson and yes, even Michael Jordan used it. I have no doubt that Kobe, who is a tremendous student of the game, "borrowed" the finger from Jordan. I truly believe "the finger" is a tremendous shooting tool. Each year I see more and more professional and collegiate players using it.

HOW LONG TO GET THE FINGER DOWN?

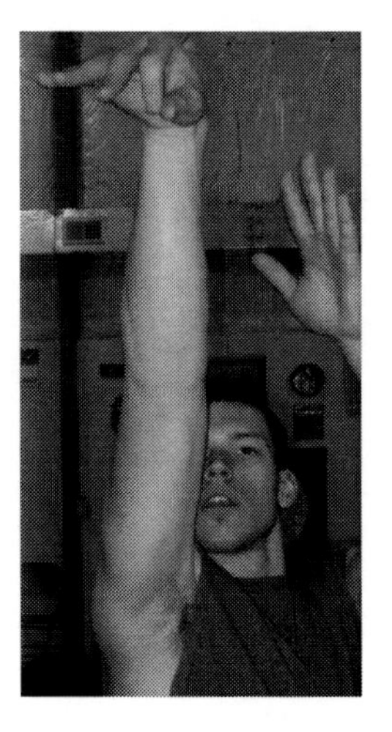

Change is difficult for young athletes to accept, especially when it concerns the most important aspect of the shot—the release. Some players embrace change immediately, while others resist new techniques. For many young athletes they can change over to the "One Finger" release within hours if they focus.

I've actually had a few open-minded students that "switched over" within minutes. Still others want to fight the concept of change and will only modify their release when they are ready. I've had a few players (thankfully this is low number) that resist the finger altogether. One high school freshman player took well over a year before he finally made this change. After he finally changed he disclosed to me, "I was so stupid. It took me a year when it should have only taken me a few days. I was hardheaded and it made me waste a full year."

DEAL OR NO DEAL

While a few of my students resist the one finger shot, there are others that can't believe they ever shot with four fingers for as long as they did. These players are not only content with the one finger method, but they refuse to even be bribed. When I'm working with new students who are resisting the one finger, I will imitate host Howie Mandel and play Deal or No Deal with my "seasoned" shooters. "I got a deal for you. I have $1,000 in the trunk of my car. If you go back to your four fingers down shot I will give you this money. But you can't use the one finger ever again. Deal or No Deal?" I have yet to find a player that will take me up on this deal. Most just laugh and add, "No way."

Some of my students have included that they wouldn't make this pact for $5,000. In other words, once a player receives the gift of the finger and accepts it, he will usually always cherish it. During one workout, I asked one of my students currently playing in the ABA if he would change his shot back to four fingers for $5,000. He laughed and said, "Coach, the finger is what will get me into the NBA."

HOLDING THE FOLLOWTHROUGH

Holding your follow-through is crucial in becoming an excellent shooter. You will not see a pure shooter who fails to hold his follow-through on each shot he attempts. If you watch the best shooters in the NBA, most of them hold it long after hitting a big shot (Reggie Miller and Kobe Bryant immediately come to mind). Holding the follow-through allows the shooter to have the same release every time. It also allows a player in training to check out his form to see if there is a problem after the shot is released. By holding your follow-through while practicing your shot and then looking at it afterward, you can figure out why you missed that shot as much as 70% of the time.

LOCKING AND RELEASING

Accurate shooting is not about where your follow-through ends up, but where you release the ball. I've seen players release their shots only slightly above their heads and continue to raise their arms and follow-throughs. They will hold their releases and ask, "Why is my shot always so flat? Look at my follow-through. My hand is above the rim." I explain to these shooters that while the follow-through looks picture perfect after the ball has been released, the release point was not where it should be.

As the shooting arm extends to shoot the ball, it must fully lock at the elbow. As it locks, the follow-through and finger takes over the shot.

THE ONE HANDED SHOT

The best shooting tool I have come across is the one-handed shooting drill (also called feather one-handed shooting drill (also called feather shooting). By shooting a few feet from the basket with one hand, this forces the shooter to stay straight and extend his release. The only difference is that the shooter must start this shot a little higher simply because he is shooting with only one hand and has no guide. If you shoot the "One Handed Drill" with a normal form, chances are fairly good the ball will roll off of the hand before you shoot it. When attempting this drill, start in a 90-degree angle so the arm looks like a capital "L."

The one handed shooting drill is a crucial drill for a shooter's success. It is very similar to a tee in baseball. Most baseball players learn to hit off of a tee when first starting out.

As players advanced on they often look at this device as a primitive tool. As they enter the major and minor leagues they quickly realize that the tee is used throughout by hitting instructors. Older basketball players often believe the one handed shooting drill is just for younger players attempting to get their mechanics down. They are very wrong.

Grant Hill easily had his best statistical year in the 1999-2000 NBA season, as he averaged 25.8 ppg. Hill had always been a decent shooter but was never mentioned in the same breath with the elite NBA shooters. During the 1999 off season he hired shooting coach, Chip Engelland to get him to the next level of shooting excellence. That summer Coach Engelland explained to Hill that his problem was that his release point was in different locations. Coach Engelland immediately put him on a steady diet of the "One Handed Shooting Drill." Each day Hill shot one-handed set shots for an hour. Soon his release became more consistent as his muscle memory improved. His 1999-2000 stats (the last season he played for the Detroit Pistons) showed remarkable improvement. His shooting percentage from the free throw line jumped from 75 to 80%. During the previous season, Hill failed to attempt a three point shot. After working on his "One Handed Shooting" for an entire summer, Grant made 34 three pointers and shot 35% from behind the arc. He made more three pointers that season than his previous five seasons combined.

GOOD MISS/BAD MISS

A proper release directs the ball to the basket. If you shoot off of the wrong fingers or your arm flails to the side you will naturally miss the side. The worst type of miss is one to the side because this shot gives you no opportunity for the ball to bounce into the rim. This is a bad miss. A good miss, on the other hand, is one that is straight, no matter if it is short or long. To become an excellent shooter, you need to first get your shot straight on every shot. Once you have accomplished this, only then should you concentrate on other aspects of shooting.

BACKSPIN

"The aerodynamic forces that result from backspin of a basketball do not appreciably affect its flight. The backspin is mostly a calibration for the shooter to produce and reproduce the same shot."

Peter J. Brancazio
Author of "The Physics of Sports"

Coaches are known to tell their players that backspin is one of the biggest aspects in determining if a shot is going to go in the basket or not. While I am not a physicist, I do believe the backspin is overrated for accurate shooting. Before I begin I would like to explain that I would rather have my players have backspin on their shot than shoot a shot that resembles a dead duck in flight. With that being said, backspin is not as important as many coaches believe.

Proper backspin on the ball is used to help it bounce into the net when it hits the rim.

Backspin does not help the shooter for more accuracy unless the player needs a soft bounce. Spinning the ball does not affect air resistance as in throwing a baseball. Basketballs generally move too slowly for this to occur.

Lastly, I am first and foremost concerned if the shot is straight. You can have all the backspin you want, but if your release is off to the side, you will miss it each and every time. I've actually heard a coach once say, "His shot is missing to the side, but look how nice that backspin looks."

THE RELEASE

If you continue working on your shooting with great focus and discipline, you will encounter a strange phenomenon that will allow you to stand on the brink of shooting greatness.

Des Flood remarked to me over two decades ago, "Coach, here's a way to recognize if one of your players is becoming an accurate shooter. Let's say one of your players shoots and because his shot is so easy and fluid he feels that he has just air-balled. He looks at his arrant shot and notices that the ball just went in the basket. In other words, if you feel like you air-balled, and you swish—you are well on your way to becoming a pure shooter."

You will read in later chapters (especially in the SWAY chapter) how effortless shooting a basketball needs to be for overall accuracy. Coach Flood was correct in that the more relaxed a player becomes (even to the point that the shot feels like an airball), the more perfect the shot will become.

WHAT DO I THINK ABOUT?

The following chapter, "AIM" will add to the release process. Please understand that the only way for a player to have a proper shooting release is to comprehend the mental approach as well as the physical technique. With out the mental side you have a vehicle lacking an engine. If you don't grasp mental concepts, your shot will be ineffective and will never get you to the places you wish to go.

CHAPTER 10 WRAP UP:

- The release is what makes the shot stay straight.
- A top-notch shooter will usually miss to the sides 5% of the time or less.
- There is no tension when you use the pinch technique. It is an easy and natural motion that will make the shot much straighter.
- It is crucial to hold your follow-through until the ball hits the rim or the net
- As the shooting arm extends to shoot, it must fully lock at the elbow. As it locks, the follow-through and finger takes over the shot.

11. AIM

"Mental is to Physical as three is to one."
Bob Knight
Basketball Hall of Fame Coach

When it comes to accurate shooting, Coach Knight may be off just a bit. The mental game becomes greater than the 3 to 1 ratio. This ratio might be as high as 7 to 1, especially when speaking about beginning shooters.

An important question that all basketball players should ask themselves is: "What do I think about when I shoot?" When I bring this question up, most high school and youth coaches are shocked that I actually want my players to think when shooting a basketball.

The most common belief by coaches is that a player (no matter what his age) should never think of anything when shooting. In other words, they believe a player's mind should always be completely void of any thoughts. This process only works for the best shooters in the world. When Kobe Bryant or Jimmer Fredette shoot, they think of nothing. Their mind is generally clear of any thoughts. These guys are professional players who have become great shooters through tremendous discipline over a great period of time. They have taken millions of practice shots during their lifetime. Young inexperienced shooters don't have the proper muscle memory, a past shooting history, or the discipline to be effective shooters without thinking about what to do during their shot. They must think or they will miserably fail.

The release is 70-80% of a shot. Therefore it only makes sense that a player should think of that part of the shot when shooting. Shooting is an aiming sport. If you aim properly, you have an opportunity to keep it straight and make it. When you shoot to the side, you have little if any chance to make the basket.

FINGER THROUGH THE RIM

The emphasis needs to be, "Finger through the rim." On every shot a shooter needs to focus and put his index finger above the rim and through it. Understand that simply because you think about putting your finger through the rim does not always mean your finger will act this way. As you well know, just because you think about an action doesn't always mean you will do that action. A good example of this is when you get angry at a person, you may think to yourself, "I would so love to pop him just one time when he's not looking." Of course being the non-violent person you are, you decide not to use fists to settle your problems. I tell my students, "Don't just think only about your finger, but be like the Nike slogan and, "'JUST DO IT!'"

Shooting a basketball without focusing on the release is similar to an individual attempting to drive a car without a steering wheel. The car might stay on the road for a few seconds, but chances are it will crash and burn. The same thing can be said regarding a shot that has a faulty follow-through because the player refuses to or forgets to focus properly each time.

EVIL VOICES AND MISDIRECTED THOUGHTS

Poor shooters think of other things than the release when shooting. The most common thought a poor shooter has is, "I have to make it," or "Don't miss." While being positive is important, you don't want to be driven by either positive or negative words. Most of the time these words come to our minds as demands as in "I have to make this!" or "This is an important shot!" Imagine taking a 50-question math test and on every question you tell yourself, "I have to get this right!" How many questions would you actually get correct? Probably very few. You obviously would put too much pressure on yourself and get questions wrong that you would normally get right. The same thing can be said when relating to shooting. If your thought process is full of demands, your body will tense up and you will miss your shot much more often than not.

When my students respond that they think about making it, I ask them, "Picture the worst shooter on your team. Now, what do you imagine they are thinking when they shoot?" The response is usually, "Making it." "Ok. Now you have the same mindset as the worst shooter you know. That would be like you wanting to be the best student in your class, but you have the same mindset as the worst student. Do you think Ray Allen (the all-time leading three-point shooter in NBA history) has the same thinking process for shooting as Shaq? If you want to be a great shooter, you can never think like the worst shooter."

DARTS, ARROWS AND DR. NAISMITH

Basketball was invented in 1891 by Dr. James Naismith, a Canadian gym instructor teaching physical education classes in Springfield, Massachusetts. Dr. Naismith wanted to offer his students a game that could be played indoors during the cold winter months and as a result basketball was invented. He was also the individual who coined the term "shooting" when attempting to put the ball in the basket. Back in those days, shooting was used only to describe what a person would do with a gun or a rifle. Dr. Naismith saw the correlation between aiming a rifle at a target and aiming at a basketball goal (or back then a peach basket).

Very few current players actually aim their shot when first learning to shoot. Most youngsters just go to their local park or driveway and aimlessly shoot without focusing. Because they lack a focus point, these young players will shoot erratically and fail much more often than they will succeed.

Shooting a basketball without a focus point is similar to going hunting with a friend in the woods. You come across a huge grizzly walking 30 yards away. "There he is. Shoot him," you tell your friend. He then proceeds to wildly fire ten shots in the next few seconds with the bullets flying all over the place including a nearby tree, into the ground, and one into your thigh.

You just shot me!" you scream at him.

"I didn't mean to," he says in an apologetic tone.

Of course the only object he failed to hit was the bear. This is the same flawed concept many youngsters use when shooting. They don't focus on the target or themselves, but instead they just shoot the ball. Of course they rarely make their shots because they don't have the correct mental approach. Just like you wouldn't want to go hunting with a friend who can't shoot straight, if you are a coach you probably don't want a player on your team who can't shoot straight either.

Shooting a basketball is an aiming sport similar to shooting a pistol, archery, and darts. Archery is an amazing sport combining power (yes, you need to be strong to pull the bow back) with great discipline and the highest degree of mental focusing. If you watch archery in the Olympics you will see these athletes shoot from over 75 yards away looking to hit a bulls-eye only a few inches in total diameter.

I have a friend who hunts wild boar with only a bow and arrow. He tells me that you only have two shots to hit the boar. Because they are vicious beasts (with big tusks weighing anywhere from 250-500 pounds), they will attack the hunter. If you don't put the boar down after 1-2 shots, chances are very good that this beast will put you down. In other words, when you hunt wild boars with only a bow and arrow you must have great focus and an even a better aim.

To become a top-notch shooter, you must understand that shooting is an aiming sport. It's similar to hunting wild boar. If you shoot to the left, the ball will travel left. Same thing can be said if the aim is to the right. If you shoot the ball straight, then chances are that it will continue to travel straight.

Quite often I use the analogy of shooting a gun and shooting a jump shot that players seem to comprehend and grasp. When shooting a basketball, the ball becomes similar to a bullet. The shooting target is the rim. Of course the player's release (especially that index finger) is similar to the rifle. What is the most important part of the shooting process? While most people believe it's the bullet or the target, it's actually the rifle. When shooting a rifle you don't say to yourself, "I hope this bullet hits the bulls-eye." You make it hit it by properly aiming. Shooting a basketball needs to have this same mental approach. If you aim your finger correctly then chances are good that it will go straight at the target.

BRING OUT THE JAWS OF LIFE!

I'm a "big boneded person" who enjoys eating donuts and drinking Dr. Pepper for breakfast. No one will ever confuse me of being a Speedo calendar model. Often times when speaking at camps I will take a seated player and ask him to stand and point directly at me ten times.

"How many times did you hit me when you pointed?" I ask the player.

"All ten" the player usually responds.

"Ok—then why is it so difficult to put your finger through that rim every single time? That rim is actually bigger than me."

I will then bring out a regulation size rim and have a player hold it as I wedge my body through it. "See, the rim is actually bigger than me. My question is simple—if you can point to me each and every time, why can you not aim your finger through an object that's even larger than me?" When it is put to the players in this manner, they realize how simple aiming the finger can actually be.

ALIENS, WITCHDOCTORS, AND DEMONS

"The finger through the rim" is a simple command, but unfocused or hardheaded athletes often fail as they attempt this easy act. Truly, I can't understand why this can be so difficult to perform correctly. Many times I will stop an unfocused player and say, "You obviously are having problems placing your finger through the rim. I have a question for you—are you possessed by demons? Were you recently abducted by aliens? Is there a witch doctor in New Guinea that has a voodoo doll that looks exactly like you?" "No" is always the response. "Then why is your shooting release out of control. I can understand that if you are possessed that it might be difficult to always put your finger through the rim. But since you don't have these problems, it should be easy to put your finger through that rim every time. RIGHT?

FROM THE BOOK OF YODA, NIKE AND HOMER

"Do, or do not. There is no try."
Jedi Master Yoda
From the Motion Picture, "Empire Strikes Back"
"Trying is the first step towards failure."
Homer Simpson
From the television show, "The Simpsons"

Throughout my travels I constantly hear the words, "But I'm *trying* to put my finger through the rim." I then think back to Yoda's infamous words that "There is no try." Basically, you either do it or you don't. People that try usually fail. As mentioned before, players should take a page from Nike and "Just do it." Put your finger through that rim every time and you will start seeing results.

GOAL ORIENTED vs. PROCESS ORIENTED

Poor shooters are goal oriented. They are consumed by results and rarely by technique. Shaquille O'Neal and Tim Duncan, both poor free throw shooters, are goal oriented at the line. Great shooters, however, have a completely different mental focus, as they are process oriented. They are much more concerned with how it feels.

One of my former students, Vlad Nieto, has a great perspective on shooting. Vlad, a former three-point specialist from Santa Ana College, commented to me on the mental portion of shooting. **"I don't care if I make it. It really doesn't bother me if I miss. What I do care about is how it feels. If it feels right, the ball will go in. It's that easy."**

KISS THE BALL IN

"There is a syndrome in sports called paralysis by analysis."
Arthur Ashe
Tennis Great, Author and Humanitarian

Poor shooters also think about other things besides positive and negative demands. I find it amusing when a player informs me that he thinks about his entire shot when shooting. When shooting any type of a shot a shooter uses hundreds of muscles, bones and tendons. If you think about your entire shot, you will have too many thoughts on your mind. The old KISS theory applies here, which is short for "Keep It Simple, Stupid." In other words, less is better and more turns the mind into a bewildered state.

"THE MAILMAN FOCUSES AND DELIVERS"

In the 1985-86 NBA season Karl Malone was a rookie for the Utah Jazz. That season he shot a dreadful 48% from the free throw line. Realizing he desperately needed help, Karl went to a sports psychiatrist seeking much needed answers. The psychiatrist asked him what he was thinking about at the free throw line which Karl responded back, "Everything."

Malone's ineffectiveness came from too much mental feedback. Because he was constantly thinking numerous thoughts, his brain was going through overload, which turned his free throw shooting into constant misses. The psychiatrist informed Karl to think of just one thought which in turn would calm his mind and his tensions. Two years later, Karl Malone had raised his season free throw percentage to 70%. He holds the NBA record for most consecutive free throws made in a playoff game (18). Malone also successfully made more career free throws than any player in NBA history. Not too bad for a player once considered a disgrace from the charity stripe.

STOP THOSE VOICES

"If you chase two rabbits both will escape."
Ancient Proverb

The common belief is that people who have numerous voices inside their heads are generally crazy. Many players fall into this demented category, especially when they step to the free throw line. A player must remember to eliminate all voices and have only one thought process in his mind when shooting. This needs to be the command, "Finger through the rim," or "Hand through the rim." But, the brain must never respond with any negative feedback.

It is impossible for a shooter to think of two different things at one time. If you don't believe this, try this mental exercise. Think of your favorite flavor of ice cream in a large bowl. Let's say it's chocolate. Now think of your favorite place in the world to go. Maybe it's on the beach in Hawaii. Now located at that beach is a large sign that reads, "NO Ice Cream on this Beach!" Can you picture both of these objects in your mind at the same time? Remember, you can't take that ice cream bowl into the beach. Think of the ice cream. Think of the beach. Chances are reasonably good that you can't picture both at the same time. Your brain does not allow this to happen. This was the problem with Karl Malone's free throw shooting during his rookie campaign. His mind was on true overload as he was thinking about too many commands at one time. Focusing on one thought is the key to proper shooting.

"I, ROBOT"

In the 2004 thriller, "I, Robot", Will Smith has a general distrust for robots. It is 20 years into the future and robots have become the custom throughout the world. It is generally believed these robots will never cause harm to humans because they are void of human emotion. It is only when one robot does discover emotion, that a murder actually takes place.

A shooter must be similar to these robots, as a player can never show any emotion at anytime. If emotion does occur (whether it's negative or positive) the shooter will greatly suffer. A shooter must think simple and have directed thoughts at all times. The only NBA pure shooter that I can recall who played with great emotion was Reggie Miler. All great shooters at that level are calm and rarely show emotion. It should be noted that Miller only showed emotion after hitting a shot and not during the shot, however.

SHOOTING SIMPLICITY

**"Basketball is like photography, if you don't focus,
all you have is the negative."**
Dan Frisby

Please understand that greatness can only be achieved by understanding the mental concepts of shooting. It should also be remembered that only the most experienced shooters cannot think of anything when they are shooting and be successful at it.

Reflect back to the first time you tried to ride a bike. Normally your first step is to ride a bike with training wheels. After you get better at it, you will take the training wheels off. The FINGER THROUGH THE RIM is just like that; only these "wheels" stay on much longer. Each player and shooter differs in how long he needs to keep these "wheels" on.

VEGAS STORY

I coach many players that when focused are outstanding shooters, and when unfocused can't hit the broad side of a barn if they were standing next to it. I am always trying to explain to my students the importance of focused shooting.

Sometimes I will ask, "What percentage of the time do you make it when you're focused and thinking of finger through the rim?" The answers I hear range anywhere from 70-90%.

Then I ask, "What percentage of the time do you make it when you're not focused; when you're NOT thinking of the finger?" The answers range from as low as 10-20%.

Then I follow up with, "Lets say you're in Las Vegas and at one table you have a 20% chance of winning and at the other table you have an 80% chance of winning. Which table would you go to?" Naturally, all players respond that the 80% table gives much better odds of winning and they would go there. "Then go to the 80% shooting table and don't leave."

CONSISTENCY

"Staying focused is the cornerstone of success."
Robert Wuhl as Arliss Michaels
From the Television Series, "Arli$$"

Being a consistent shooter begins with mentally focusing each time you step onto a basketball court. Too often I come across players whose mental focus changes from day to day. One afternoon the player will be focused and thinking of "finger through the rim" on each shot he takes. The results are usually swish after swish. The next day, the player will be unfocused and therefore the player misses wildly to the sides.

How did this happen? Did the body drastically change over night? Was the player abducted by aliens? The answer of course is that the mental focusing changed in this shooter. If you look at a player who constantly rides the daily shooting rollercoaster of tremendous highs and extreme lows, all you have to do to find the answers is look no further than the mind.

BRAIN TYPES

In spring, 2000 I was introduced to the book, "The Key to Sports Success", by Jon Niednagel. I had seen Niednagel on a few sports shows and had taken an interest in his "brain typing" concept. Niednagel was a former youth soccer coach from Southern California who transformed the Briggs Meyers personality test and adjusted it so it would work effectively for athletes. Soon professional teams were calling him and asking him to evaluate players before draft day and near trading deadlines.

Niednagel became famous when he publicly announced that Peyton Manning would be a Hall of Fame player and Ryan Leaf would be a huge disappointment (drafted as the second player in the 2000 NFL draft; he would be out of the league within three seasons). Among the NBA franchises that have used his services are: the Boston Celtics, Minnesota Timberwolves and the Phoenix Suns.

"The Key to Sports Success" has changed how I view athletics and the way I coach athletes. Niednagel claims that there are 16 different brain types with eight being introverted and eight being extroverted. Through a simple test, you can see what your brain type is. Niednagel believes, for example, many of the best quarterbacks have the same brain type. NBA point guards, meanwhile, generally only have four of the possible sixteen brain types.

I always wondered why some players instantly catch on and others take what is seems like forever to understand a simple shooting technique. It bothered me that some high school players could not understand what I wanted, but a third grader could completely grasp these same concepts within minutes. Niednagel's "brain typing" greatly helped me to understand that each player thinks and learns at a different pace and overall level.

INTROVERTS vs. EXTRAVERTS

Introverted players make much better shooters than extraverted players. The main reason lies in the fact that introverts will get into a gym, go to a basket where there is no one and shoot by themselves for hours.

Extraverts have a completely different mindset. They need to be around other people. Extraverts are much more likely to get into a gym, start talking to players at a basket and end up challenging anyone to a one on one or two on two game. I lived with an extreme extravert trying to make the basketball team at a local junior college. He spent a great deal of time at the local gym, but did not on his shooting due to the fact he never worked on his shot longer than five minutes at a time. His shot improved only after he finally developed enough discipline to shoot by himself with focus.

When I researched many of the best shooters in the NBA history, I discovered a good majority often are introverts including: Kobe Bryant, Larry Bird, Michael Jordan, Steve Kerr, Steve Nash, Jerry West, Chris Mullin and Jeff Hornacek. Most European players (Dirk Nowitski and Peja Stojakovic immediately come to mind) are introverted and excellent shooters.

Extraverts can become quality shooters in time, but only occurs through discipline. Magic Johnson is considered one of the greatest extraverts in NBA history. He came into the league as an average shooter, but became a solid three-point threat. In the 1988-89 season, Magic took his shooting talents to a new level as he led the NBA in free throw shooting. He spent many thousands of hours honing his shooting talents to get where he achieved in the second half of his professional career. Magic is a rare breed among extraverts, however. Few extroverts have patience and discipline to become pure shooters.

CHAPTER 11 WRAP UP:

- The release is 70-80% of a shot, therefore it only makes sense a player should think of that part of the shot when shooting.
- Shooting is an aiming sport.
- The most common thought is, "I have to make it," or "Don't miss."
- Poor shooters are goal oriented. In other words, they are consumed by results.

12. RHYTHMIC HOP

"I feel the need... the need for speed!"
Tom Cruise as Maverick
From the Motion Picture, "Top Gun"

The lower body mechanics of shooting are simple. The more a person bends his knees, the slower the shot becomes. Also, if a shooter bends his knees too much, he will lose needed power. Please understand that I don't want my players to shoot like Frankenstein from the waist down either. Players need to always flex their knees but should NEVER bend them.

A pogo stick gets all of its spring from its bottom. It has no knees. A shooter must also get a great majority of his spring from the bottom—the toes. Watch a quick shooter and I guarantee that he has quick and "soft" feet. If you can hear a player's feet when taking a jump shot, he either has extremely heavy feet or is bending his knees too much. A stomping or a squeaking sound should never be heard when taking a shot.

Stomping or a loud thud means the shooter is using too much lower body power on his shot. It is not about power but instead, quickness. The louder the feet, the longer I twill take to shoot. Also, if you hear a squeaking motion, this shows the player is trying to dig himself into the ground. In baseball it is important to dig the batter into the batter's box. The batter's box is comprised of dirt and becomes crucial that the player digs in for better traction. In basketball, however, the court is made of wood, concrete or blacktop. A shooter has perfect traction on these surfaces and therefore never needs to dig in.

LOWER BODY MECHANICS: "BEND THOSE KNEES!"

This is the most overused saying in shooting, basketball and perhaps in all of sports. If you bring together a group of coaches and ask them "Name one of the two most important concepts of shooting," I guarantee one response will be, "Bending the knees."

A player does not shoot with his knees, however.. If a player or coach believes the knees are the most important aspect of shooting, then they should attempt to kick the ball into the basket using only the knees. I have often wondered why the idea of bending knees has become so prevalent throughout the teaching process of shooting. After all, there are no pure shooters in college or the professional ranks that fully bend their knees and squat when shooting. Finally, it dawned on me why the knees are always mentioned when discussing shooting. Back in the origins of basketball, players used a two-handed push motion when shooting. Thankfully, no one shoots this way anymore but unfortunately and amazingly, this concept is still being taught today.

The two-handed push shot was a difficult task to perform. It took a great amount of energy just to get an open shot off. The energy from this shot was derived primarily from the legs and especially the knees. This is where the term, "Bend those knees" originally came from. The idea of bending the knees was been handed down from generation to generation of coaches and players.

THE BALANCE FACTOR

Since the first moment that I picked up a basketball I was told by my coaches that a shooter's feet must be squared to the basket in order to have balance. Pointing your feet to the basket, however, has little to do with your balance. Lower body balance concerns the player's width between their feet. If your feet are too wide apart or too close together, you will lose your balance in shooting.

Try this technique and you will definitely understand shooting balance. Square up with your feet pointed directly to the basket and have a player next to you push on your shoulders. You should move very little. Now point your feet to the right if you're a right hander (opposite for a lefty) and have the player once again push on you in the same manner. In both occasions you should have moved very little. To perfect your lower body base, focus more on the overall width and less on the direction of the feet. You will find a greater balance this way.

WIDTH OF LEGS

The best shooters in the world are narrow shooters. The worst shooters are generally WIDE shooters. I know that goes against everything that many coaches teach, but it's true.

The notion that a player's base should be "shoulder width" is universally accepted. There is only one problem with this. The shoulder width concept is flawed and doesn't work.

If you watch the best shooters, their base is usually 1-3 inches apart. You can see this with Kobe Bryant, Jameer Nelson, JJ Redick, JR Smith, Carmelo Anthony and Deron Williams just to name a few. The same can be said for the best women shooters as well.

The "shoulder width" concept fails to work because it is not comfortable and it hurts overall speed and balance. Man does not walk in a shoulder width position and he definitely doesn't stand this way. So why do coaches continually teach it? Simply, they don't know better. The shoulder width concept has been around for 60 years and many coaches refuse to believe that basketball has changed. Jerry West, Bill Bradley, Larry Bird, Rick Barry and Oscar Robertson never shot in a shoulder-width position and they became pretty decent players to say the least.

Unless the player is truly bowlegged, having a shoulder width shot does not help a shot and actually hurts in balance and overall speed. If you have a wide base the motion actually turns into a jump stop, which forces the shot to become slower and stiffer.

Lastly, having a wide shot can have long lasting effects on the knee region. Girl and woman athletes tear their Anterior Crucial Ligament (ACL) 4-8 times more than that of boys/men. In basketball girls have a tendency of having wider bases than boys as well. You can see this especially when a girl shoots. I believe each time a girl with a wide shot actually shoots, she is straining the knee ligaments and muscles. For these girls I believe it is just a matter of time before tears and strains develop.

"Hey, I'm no orthopedic surgeon – know what I'm sayin'? But this can't be good."

Last year I spoke with a head girls high school varsity basketball coach from Ohio. I asked him how the season was going and he responded, "Terrible Coach. I lost three starters to ACL tears."

I then asked him, "Do those girls shoot wide?"

"Yes. They are very wide shooters." And there lies the reason for the terrible season.

THE NEED IS SPEED!!

"Speed is what you need. You need speed!"
Burgess Meredith as Mickey
From the Motion Picture, "Rocky II"

On a jump shot, the lower body is built for speed and not for power. We have already discussed the problems with bending your knees too much. It slows your shot down and therefore allows the defense to easily guard you.

The lower body of shooting is a plyometric activity. In the 1970's, the Eastern Bloc countries discovered a way of training to increase speed, agility and jump ability that is currently used today throughout the NBA, college, and at many high schools. When most young athletes think of the term plyometrics they immediately visualize exercises that will make them jump out of the gym. While it will help your vertical, it is also designed to make your feet quicker and give you "harmony and rhythm." Pylometrics are exercises where the muscle is contracted eccentrically then immediately concentrically. In other words, the muscle is stretched before it is contracted. The results are a quicker motion and less knee bend is needed.

Becoming a quick shooter begins with the speed of the toes hitting the floor and springing back up. If the toes have a tendency to stay on the floor for a long period of time, more leg muscles are needed with a great majority coming from the knees. Of course, this means the shot will become slower. If the toes hit the surface and immediately pounce back up, then there is less leg muscle needed which makes the shot quicker.

Many young players don't understand the importance of having a quick shot. I ask my students, "Would you rather have a slow good jump shot or a quick poor jump shot?" Most immediately respond that they would rather have a good shot that's slow. "Think about it," I respond. "If you have a slow but accurate shot you can't do a whole lot with it. What are you going to do, go around and put on shooting demonstrations? But if you have a quick shot, you will be able to get your shot off at any time." Speed is crucial in shooting. A quick shot and you can get off 20-25 shots a game. If you have a slow shot you might be lucky if you average 2-3 shots per game. Having a quick jump shot is everything!

BE A QUICK JUMPER

"As a rule, bona fide leapers are not good shooters and they have less range."
Stu Lantz
Basketball Analyst

The more a player bends his knees, the slower the shot becomes. If you watch the quickest shooters in the NBA and WNBA, they don't use very little knee flexion. Ray Allen is the quickest shooter in the NBA and has been that way for over a decade. So why is Allen such a quick shooter? He is not the youngest nor is he one of the best athletes. The speed of his jump is based around that he is a 100% toe jumper. He springs up similar to the spring on a pogo stick. He has little if any bend of his knees as well.

If you want to see players that jump high on their shot, just go to your local park. You will come across lots of these "playground warriors." These players jump high on the shot by overly bending their knees. This leads to a slower and rigid shot.

Many people believe that a player needs to use a great deal of leg power because it is termed a "jump shot." In other words, quite a few players and coaches believe jump means to jump as high as you can. In basketball there are power jump shooters and rhythm and speed jump shooters. Give me a team full of rhythm and speed shooters over a team of power jump shooters and we'll beat you by 30 every time. The power jump shooter first of all has a difficult time getting his shot off. If you think of Larry Bird, he barely got any elevation on his shot. What he did was possess a smooth upper body release and a deceivingly pair of quick feet.

KINGPIN AND QUICK FEET

One of my favorite comedy movies is the Farrelly Brothers, "Kingpin." Woody Harrelson plays Roy Munson, a down and out ex-professional bowler who through a mishap has been confined to being a bowling supply salesman. One day as he's trying to sell supplies in a second rate-bowling alley he comes across an Amish recreational bowler, Ishmael Boorg

(played by Randy Quaid). Roy approaches Ishmael and tells him all the things he did wrong on his approach and release.

"You can tell all that by just seeing me throw one strike?" Ishmael asks.

"I didn't see it. I heard it," Roy responds back.

When it comes to the lower body, you can hear what players are doing right and wrong. If you can't hear the feet, chances are that shooter has quick feet. If you hear a stomp or a squeak, the player generally has slow feet or is struggling with his feet.

LOWER BODY FORM:

There are generally three ways to shoot a jump shot with different lower body movements. I will explain all three and then I will detail when you should and shouldn't use each of these methods.

THE STANDSTILL SHOT

The standstill shot is exactly as the name sounds. The player receives the pass, gathers himself and shoots the ball in a standstill motion. To get more power, the player may have to bend his knees. Because the athletes have become so much quicker, the standstill shot technique has become more and more obsolete in the past 25 years. I don't recommend this shooting method. In the standstill shooter, there is little if any rhythm. This shot can be difficult to not only get the shot off without getting it blocked, but for the weaker players it can be almost impossible to reach the rim.

This is a fairly outdated shot, but still is used by slower and taller players. Magic Johnson had a standstill shot. He could get away with it because he was a 6'9" point guard in an age that most lead guards were no taller than 6'4". Magic also had the luxury of playing alongside the greatest scorer in NBA history, Kareem Abdul-Jabbar and various all-stars and quality shooters that included: Byron Scott, James Worthy, Jamaal Wilkes, Norm Nixon and Michael Cooper. With such a great arsenal of outside shooters and the big guy down low, it was difficult to double team Magic. If he had played with lesser talent throughout his career, Magic would have had to rely only on his drive or develop a quicker jump shot.

THE 1-2 STEP SHOT

The 1-2 step occurs when a player catches the ball in a staggered stance. Upon receiving the ball, the back foot steps forward making both feet fairly equal. With both feet down, the shooter next jumps up and releases the ball. The 1-2 step is the most taught lower body form with at least 90% of all high school coaches teaching this method. The reason this shot is such a high number is the reason that so many coaches teach to bend their knees when shooting.

The 1-2 step is "old school" and because today's coaches were taught this method at an early age, they figure that it must be the correct way to shoot. Coaches are people of habit that usually accept what is universally taught and never question the norm. There are times that a player can properly use the 1-2 step. For the most part, it is a technique that is based around power and strength and can be effectively used coming off screens.

There are some aspects that I don't like with the 1-2 step, however. The most important aspect deals with the overall speed of the shot. With athletes becoming quicker and faster, it is necessary to construct a quicker shot. The 1-2 step makes it harder for a player to get proper rhythm. Shooting is one of the most rhythmic activities an athlete can perform. One little shooting error from a player and the shot will usually end in a miss. With the 1-2 step technique, the shot is led by stepping with two feet at different times. There is little balance and even less rhythm when shooting with the 1-2 step.

THE HOP SHOT

Many coaches look at "the hop" and fail to notice that it is widely accepted in international basketball and the NBA, and will make comments like, "That's not how you shoot." When I first learned about shooting from Coach Des Flood, I noticed he never spoke about the lower body. I asked him one day, "Coach, you never speak about the legs and feet. It's always the upper body. Why is that?"

"The upper body is where you get your accuracy," Coach Des responded. The lower body is taught so many ways by so many team coaches. If I teach my students to shoot one way with the lower body, chances are his coach will teach him the other way. I don't want to confuse any of my shooters."

I don't know if that was a warning from Coach Des, but he was correct in his belief. Numerous times I have produced great shooters over a summer in which I have ingrained in their psyche the importance of the hop. They become quick and accurate shooting machines and they go back to high school basketball in September and their coach exclaims, "What the hell is that? Who taught you that? Go back to stepping into your shot." One time a club coach actually told me "No one in the NBA hops into their shot."

If you only teach the upper body techniques of shooting and neglect the lower body, you are serving the pizza void of any toppings. I would rather teach the whole shot and take a risk that the player's high school coach will either be a "hop" coach or will not teach any aspect of the feet and legs in shooting. It should be known that while I strongly urge using the hop, I do also teach the 1-2 to give a player some knowledge and understanding if he does get a coach that makes him step into his shot.

THE GREAT DEBATE—1-2 vs. THE HOP

As players advance to the collegiate level and the professional ranks, the HOP is used more often. Former University of Arizona Head Coach Lute Olson also believes in the hop. Elected to the Basketball Hall of Fame in 2002, Coach Olson makes his players hop in practice or they have to run. Already having a few of my shooters play at

U of A, I began working with Ricky Anderson soon after his high school senior season was completed. I informed him that Coach Olson expects all of his players to hop into their shot. Ricky would return after his freshman year at Arizona. "Paul (Ricky is one of only a handful of people that refers to me by my first name), I want to thank you for working with me on the hop. That helped me so much. You were right in what they teach and because I knew it going in, I didn't have to run."

If you watch closely in the NBA you will notice the smallest players—players from 5-10 to 6-4—predominately hop on their shot. Why? Because it is faster. The players that need to have the quickest shots are always the guards because of their lack of size. These players include: Ray Allen, Kembo Walker. Jimmer Fredette, JJ Redick, Jameer Nelson, Monte Ellis, Deron Williams, Stephan Curry, Derrick Rose and Chauncey Billups

NBA Players in the 6-5 to 6-8 height range are normally both 1-2 and hop shooters. In other words, sometimes they hop and other times they 1-2 step. Lebron James, Dwayne Wade, Kobe and Michel Jordan are in this category.

Lastly, players that are 6-9 and tall generally are 1-2 step shooters. Because of their size, they can be slower than the guards in regards to the speed of their shot. It should be noted, however, that Oklahoma City All-Star, Kevin Durant is 6-9 but is a hop shooter and has one of the quickest shots. Because his shot is so quick, he has become perhaps the deadliest threat in the NBA leading the league in scoring for two consecutive seasons (2009-2010 and 2010-2011). I do not believe he would be as much of a threat if he was only a 1-2 step shooter.

Obviously, all high school and youth coaches should sit down at a television set and watch these top shooters and see how these players are using their lower body when it comes to shooting. Unfortunately, most coaches when they watch a game don't watch a shooter's footwork, but instead they examine the offensive sets and the overall defensive play. They watch basketball as a team coach and rarely as a shooting or skills instructor.

"THE HOP BOUNCES INTO CLIPPER CAMP"

Craig Hodges is considered one of the greatest shooters in basketball history. Hodges and Larry Bird (pretty good company to be with) are the only three-time winners of the NBA three point shooting contest. His mark of 29 points in the shootout is still a record. Hodges, a big advocate of the hop method, told me a story about his rookie season with the San Diego Clippers.

Hodges, a second round pick from Cal State Long Beach, was effectively going through the Clippers shooting drills when rookie head coach, Paul Silas stopped the drill. Silas, a former 1-2 shooter during his playing days with the Boston Celtics, couldn't figure out how Hodges was getting his shot off so quickly. The year was 1980 and the hop was just being introduced by a handful of players throughout the NBA.

Silas and the coaching staff couldn't understand how Hodges was able to get his shot off on taller and more experienced players. After a few minutes Silas informed Hodges to actually slow the shot down so they could better see what was taking place in his lower body. After closer review the Clippers staff realized the Hop technique was the true reason that Craig Hodges' shot was so quick.

QUIET FEET AND STAY ON YOUR TOES

As we have already discussed, a shooter's feet should be quiet and void of noise. The quieter and "softer" the feet are, the quicker the shooter is. If you would attend an NBA game and sit near courtside, chances are fairly good that you will not hear the best shooters feet when they pull-up or when they come off a screen. If you listen to a poor shooter, on the other hand, you will often hear a stomping motion.

It is important that your feet point down when you shoot. I have had many players that come to me for the first time and try to shoot in a heel-toe manner or flat footed. In other words, they use their heals to enter a jump shot which also includes their first few dribbles on a pull-up. If you see a slow player, pay attention to his feet and how he runs. Chances are good that he runs in a heal/toe manner. I have never seen a great athlete, a dominating guard or a pure shooter run heal/toe.

This can often times be difficult for players to change. Most of these players have walked and run this way all of their lives and many will find it difficult to change. Using different instruments and techniques to strengthen your toes and help with your overall muscle memory can greatly assist. These can include a jump rope, simply walking on your toes, toe raises, and using Strength Shoes or Jumpsoles. Strength Shoes and Jumpsoles are excellent aids to achieving quicker feet and better overall speed. These devices that came out on the market in the early 90's, are worn on the feet (Strength Shoes are shoes, while Jumpsoles are slipped on over the shoe). The premise is fairly simple—both eliminate the heel and put all the pressure on the balls of the feet. By doing this in a repetitive motion, strength in the calf will build which will lead to overall quicker feet and a more explosive player.

LEGS LEAD TO YOUR SHOULDERS

In the next chapter we will discuss the importance of relaxing your shoulders and neck when you shoot. The shoulders are a series of muscles, bones and tendons that wish to relax and always be free. Unfortunately your brain wants to control the shoulders. Thus, we have a huge dilemma here with a part that wants to control and a part that survives only on freedom.

The lower body can greatly assist your shoulders to give it needed freedom and elevate pressure and tension. Whichever direction the feet go, the shoulders will do the opposite. If the feet are behind the shooter, the shoulders will naturally lean in a forward motion. When the feet are in front of the shooter, the shoulders will naturally sway back. You will read further the importance of not shooting in a straight up and down motion. When this occurs (even though the good majority of coaches teach it), the shooter will tense his shoulders and neck and actually will lose needed strength for accuracy.

If the shooter leads slightly with his feet, the shoulders will become relaxed in a natural position. By jumping only a few inches forward, the shoulders automatically relax and allow the shot to be free of tension and pressure. When a player jumps in a vertical position and does not lead with the feet first, it becomes difficult to properly rotate the shoulders back.

When you think about it, shooting with your feet slightly in front of you makes perfectly sense. Imagine how you walk. A person walks with his feet somewhat in front of him and his shoulders slightly arched back because it feels comfortable and is more efficient in getting where he wishes to go. If he walked, however, with his feet directly vertical from the rest of his body, he would become tense and slow. His steps would naturally be shortened which would make his walk appear sluggish. If you lead with our feet when we walk because it is comfortable, then why wouldn't we use this same means when shooting? It just makes obvious sense.

THE PULLUP JUMPER

The footwork of a pull-up jump shot must be somewhat similar to the way you would spring off a diving board. Imagine running on a diving board and springing off it into a jump shot. This becomes the footwork for a pull-up. Remember that when you use a diving board you do not fall off it, but instead you jump off of it.

On the pull-up jump shot it is important to run on your toes. A good drill to work on your pull-up and your footwork is to start from half court and run into the shot without dribbling. There are many coaches who believe that by not dribbling, I am actually teaching my players bad habits that include traveling, but this couldn't be further from the truth. When players dribble, they have an inclination of worrying more about the dribble and less about the shot's form, the speed of the shot, and footwork. When we eliminate the dribble, players have a tendency to use more toes and get a quicker hop. Only until the player masters the pull-up without the dribble do we then allow the shooter to use the dribble.

"LEARN FROM MY MISTAKES"

The pull-up jump shot can be one of the greatest tools a player can possess. It allows a player to be creative and gives a player another important arsenal in his weaponry. In July 2004 I ran into Tracy Murray at the Fila Summer Pro League at Cal State University Long Beach. Tracy, a 16 year NBA player, has long been known as one of the top shooters in the NBA. In the 1993/94 season, Tracy led the NBA in three-point field goal percentage. Tracy saw that I had a few young players with me and said, "Fellows, here's an important tip. Always work on your pull-up jump shot. It's what will make you great."

Sometimes your own failures can give you great insight that you try to pass on to others. What my young players did not know was that Tracy Murray came into college and the NBA as a standstill shooter that could not create and use the pull-up effectively. I coached against Tracy Murray in the late 80's and early 90's in the "Say

No" Summer Collegiate League at Cal State University Los Angeles. At that time Tracy was a standout player at UCLA, known as a pure shooter. We never, however, really worried about Tracy hurting us. My tactic was to make sure that Tracy's defender would never leave him open and then once he caught the ball, to suffocate him so he would have to put it on the floor. The last thing we would ever want to do was leave Tracy open for a jump shot. We, however, never respected his pull-up like his pure shot off the pass.

Our strategy worked as he struggled to hit double figures in scoring. His teammate, Chris Mills, is a player we could never stop because he had an unbelievable pull up jump shot. Mills, who headlined for University of Arizona and would later have a 10 year NBA career, scored 40+ each time we would play them, primarily because of his effective pull-up. I learned the hard way that a player with a pull-up (like Chris Mills) will be more efficient than a stand still shooter (like Tracy Murray).

THE HOP OFF THE PASS

The easiest way to remember what to do on the jump shot is when the pass is in the air, your body should also be in the air. You will catch the ball in the air, your feet will hit the floor, and then you will instantly spring up. When catching the pass, make sure that you catch the ball at the top of your jump or as you're descending to that point. It is important that you don't catch the ball as you're coming down.

Most players naturally believe that it makes more sense to catch the pass as you are on your downward flight. The belief that if you shorten your hop, your shot will become quicker is incorrect. By shortening the bounce, you will be forced to use additional power, which of course means bending your knees.

DON'T FIGHT THE GRAVITY

While you feel gravity taking over on your hop, don't ever fight it. Taking an extra inch or two hop does not generally help your shot and can actually throw your balance off. Don't be hard headed when this occurs. When you feel this gravitational pull, allow your feet to bounce down at that instance. Gravity will always win out in the long run.

SPEED AND THE MIND

Obviously the quicker the shot, the less a player will over think. The slower the shot is the longer he will have to think what he should or shouldn't do. Obviously over thinking will also lead a shooter to become tense and apprehensive. Shooting quickly not only greatly helps in getting the ball off faster so the defender becomes incapable of blocking the shot, but it also greatly aids in remaining focused and confident.

CHAPTER 12 WRAP UP:

- The more a person bends his knees, the slower the shot becomes. Also, if the shooter bends too much, he will actually lose power
- Flex your knees. Do not bend them.
- A shooter gets a great majority of its spring from his toes.
- Watch a quick shooter and I can almost guarantee that they have quick and "soft feet."
- Pointing your feet to the basket has little to do with your balance, however. True lower body balance is all about the player's width in his feet.
- On a jump shot, the lower body is built for speed and not for power. The lower body of shooting is a plyometric.
- To become a quick shooter begin with the speed of the toes hitting the floor and springing back up.
- "The Hop" is much quicker and has greater overall balance than stepping into the shot, especially when it concerns the pull-up

13. THE TURN

Many coaches constantly scream to their players, "Square your feet!" According to some coaches, squaring the feet toward the basket is the most important aspect in all of shooting. I've actually heard coaches proclaim to their players, "If you don't square your feet, you won't shoot correctly."

For many years I subscribed to this philosophy that all players must square their feet to have total balance (I also call it ten toes to the basket). While I had some good shooters come through my shooting program, I was never fully satisfied. After all, very few of my students looked similar to the pure shooters playing at the NBA, WNBA and college levels. In May 2005 this would dramatically change.

During this time I was coaching in Calgary, Canada and working often with sophomore, Irving Chong. Irving, an excellent listener and shooter, was having difficulties with a tense pair of shoulders. He was shooting in a straight up and down manner and was constantly finishing short on his shot. I was noticing that his feet were turning slightly to the side as he shot.

"Irving, try to square your feet," I responded. He attempted to square his feet over the next 10 minutes with disastrous results. Finally I asked him to return to his jump shot with feet turned sideways. This time, however, I asked Irving to focus on squaring his shooting shoulder. With one adjustment, Irving's shoulder tension disappeared and he instantly looked like a college or NBA shooter.

When I returned back to my home later that afternoon I watched various NBA video tapes and started looking at internet pictures of the best shooters in basketball (past and present). Much to my surprise I discovered the best shooters did not have ten toes to the basket, but instead were turned with the shooting shoulder and hip squared to the basket. Could I have finally found the missing shooting ingredient that I had been looking so long for?

This discovery intrigued me. After all, I had been "brainwashed" by my coaches from an early age that EVERY player must square his feet when shooting. After reviewing various video tapes and pictures, I grabbed my basketball and drove to the nearest gym to investigate further.

SEARCHING FOR THE TRUTH

There were so many questions and few answers. Why did these players turn their feet and square their shooting shoulders? Doesn't this hurt their overall lower body balance? As I began shooting with the new techniques, many of the questions would soon be answered. The more I shot with my shoulder squared, the better the shot felt. By the end of the afternoon, I completely understood that there are three reasons why a player should lead with his shoulder.

The first reason to use this shooting method is that it helps to align the shot. The human body is built with the shoulder and arm on the side of the athlete. Stand at the free throw line with your feet lined up to the basket. This is how a player is supposed to shoot according to most coaches. Now put your arms down to your side and raise your shooting arm in a straight manner. You will notice that your hand is off to the side 3-inches in comparison to the rim. Because you shoot a jump shot from the side of your body, your shot will always be a few inches off by shooting in this manner.

The second reason lies with the concept of shoulder and neck tension. When a player shoots with his feet facing the basket, he will naturally become a two shoulder shooter. In other words, both shoulders will be used almost equally when shooting. When a player dominates with both shoulders while shooting, both shoulder blades will therefore dig into that player's neck. When this happens tension is immediately formed. Many inconsistent shooters will have great shoulder and neck tension resulting in a shot that is constantly short or long. By dominating with one shoulder the tension is decreased and shooting becomes much easier to perform. Your non shooting shoulder should always be relaxed and void of tension. Great shooters do not have this tension simply because they are one shoulder shooters. If you do continue to have tension after switching to squaring your shoulder to the basket, please review the shoulder and neck chapter.

Lastly, squaring the shoulder helps in reducing overall shooting movement. When a player shoots with two shoulders, he has a large range of movement. When squaring the shoulder, however, this range of movement is greatly reduced. For inconsistent and often times "wild" shooters, this greatly helps to become more accurate.

Please note the feet position should not be turned in a drastic position. The best way to explain feet position is to imagine your body like a dial on a wrist watch. The feet should be turned to around 10 pm for right handed players and 2 pm for lefties. Each player is different, however. Ray Allen is at 11 pm and Larry Bird was at 9 pm (a drastic turn to say the least). Use the 10 pm and 2 pm as a guide, but you can always adjust to what best suits you.

ONLY IN SHOOTING

Since I was a youngster I have been brainwashed that I must have my feet perfectly squared to the basket. Perhaps the biggest "sin" in all of basketball is to not square your feet when shooting. If you think about it, shooting is the only skill in all of sports where you have your feet turned towards a target. Turning your feet and leading with your dominant shoulder are found in the following sports: throwing a football or baseball, putting in golf, bowling, archery, darts and firing a gun at a target. Perhaps if basketball coaches across North America adopted the lead shoulder concepts from these other aiming sports, good shooters then wouldn't be so few and far between.

The one shoulder alignment is a theory that shooting experts Dave Hopla and Tom Norland teach. Both of these highly respected coaches instruct their players to square their dominant shoulder in order to alleviate tension and for better alignment to the basket. Both Hopla and Norland fully understand that shooting is not an activity that constitutes squaring your feet to the basket.

SELLING THE IDEA

As I have mentioned before, if you look closely at the top shooters playing at the professional or college levels, you will notice that they don't square their feet. After all, haven't we seen Kobe Bryant with his body turned sideways and fading out of bounds hit shot after shot? But according to most coaches this should result in a miss. Right? Wrong!

While I understand the NBA is entertainment, I still realize that many of the best shooters in the world are playing in the NBA. I've heard high school and youth coaches utter to their players, "Don't watch the NBA. It's garbage. You'll get nothing out of it." While I do agree that college basketball is more pure and fundamentally based, I can't agree with these coaches. It would definitely be worth a player's time to just watch the NBA for the purpose of viewing great shooters and how they actually get their shots off.

By analyzing the shooting motions of great shooters from today and yesterday, you can clearly see what should and shouldn't be taught. If you watch Michael Jordan, Carmelo Anthony, Kobe Bryant, Stephan Curry, JJ Redick and other excellent shooters you will notice that they lead with their dominant shoulder and yes, their feet are slightly turned sideways.

I never have to sell this notion to the players. All I have to do is ask them they following: "Have you ever seen Kobe Bryant shoot? Does he shoot with two shoulders or one?" At this point I demonstrate the difference between a one shoulder shooter that squared his shooting shoulder and a two shoulder shooter that squares his feet. The player always responds that Kobe shoots with one shoulder. "What about Jimmer Fredette? Or Paul Pierce? Or Dirk Nowitski? They all shoot with one shoulder? RIGHT? But you shoot with two."

Later, I will show various action pictures that I have collected from college and NBA players that clear show these players dominating their shot with their shooting shoulder. The kids are usually an "easy sell." When you explain it to the parents in detail, they are very accepting. Unfortunately, coaches can often times be narrow minded concerning new changes, especially when it concerns squaring the feet. They have been teaching this concept for so long that there can be great hesitancy to change.

WHERE DID IT ALL BEGIN?

NBA players have been turning their feet and aligning their shooting shoulder since the 60's. The first two players to noticeably turn while shooting a jump shot were Oscar Robertson and Jerry West. These two hardwood icons are also considered two of the greatest shooters in basketball history as well. During the late 60's and early 70's other great shooters used this technique as well including Bill Bradley, Pete Maravich and Walt Frazier. The 70's and 80's would produce other outstanding feet turned/shoulder aligned shooters including Chris Mullin, Larry Bird, Byron Scott and Danny Ainge.

In my travels I encountered the Indiana Basketball Hall of Fame in New Castle, Indiana. As I browsed through the Hall I came across a few action pictures of Oscar Robertson playing for Crispus Attucks High School in the late 1950's. As I looked closer at the pictures I noticed every single one had the Big O shooting with his feet turned. Robertson is still regarded to this day as one of the greatest guards to ever step foot on the hardwood at the collegiate and professional levels. He revolutionized the guard position (he averaged a triple double for an entire year) and he along with Jerry West changed the way the best shooters currently shoot.

DO AS I SAY...NOT AS I DO

Many look at NBA players as experts in their field, but I am quite amazed at how many we encounter that are excellent shooters and scorers and yet they don't truly understand the mechanics of "the turn."

In Better Basketball Videos, JJ Redick speaks in great detail regarding squaring your feet to the basket. Oh, but there is a problem here. No one in the NBA turns more than Redick (see picture). So he other "sold out" to be the spokesperson of the shooting portion of Better Basketball videos or he doesn't realize that he turns when he shoots. I truly believe that he thinks he is squared to the basket when he is shooting.

In Homework Basketball, "Pistol" Pete Maravich also discusses the notion of squaring your feet to the basket. He explains that an important aspect of shooting is to square your feet and the proceeds to demonstrate by turning his feet.

I believe Redick and Maravich both believed that they squared their feet when shooting. I also believe that there are many players in the NBA and WNBA that naturally turn their feet, but fail to fully realize that they are doing this.

THE ONE EYED SHOOTER

When a player shoots with feet squared to the basket, he ultimately becomes a two shoulder shooter. When this occurs, he will in the process become a "two shooter." In other words, he can see the basket with both eyes. His shooting arm will normally be next to the side of his jaw and earlobe. When a player shoots by leading with his shooting shoulder, (which forces the feet to slightly turn) he will become a one eye shooter. The shooting form is in front of the player instead of at his side, which will block out the shooting eye (right eye for right handed players, left eye for left handed) when releasing the shot. It is vital that a player becomes a one eye shooter because it will keep the arm and the shot straight. If you are a two eye shooter chances are quite high that you miss a good percentage of your shots to the side.

The best shooters in the world are one eyed shooters. As they shoot they go through the jaw, the cheek and finally their shooting eye (right eye for right handers). Watch a poor shooter closely. Chances are that player will shoot in a two eye motion with their shooting arm usually past their ear. It is almost impossible to make this shot as the shot now will veer off to the side.

CHAPTER 13 WRAP UP:

- Squaring your shooting hip and shoulder helps to align the shot while alleviating tension in neck.
- When a player dominates with both shoulders while shooting, both shoulder blades will therefore dig into that player's neck causing tension.
- NBA players have been turning their feet and aligning their shooting shoulder since the 60's.
- The best shooters in the world are one eyed shooters.
- It is vital that a player becomes a one eye shooter because it will keep the arm and the shot straight.

14. SWAY

The difference between a poor shooter and an average shooter is in the release. The difference, however, between an average shooter and a great shooter lies in the individual's shoulders and neck region. This is easily the second most crucial area concerning shooting as well.

We've already discussed many misconceptions concerning shooting that are taught in most basketball camps, teams and programs in the United States. One of the greatest concerns is the notion that a player should always shoot straight up and down. This may be the most ludicrous shooting misconception of all. In short, the human body is not designed to only go in an up and down position.

In the movie "Hoosiers", Gene Hackman (playing Coach Norman Dale) explains to his team, "You are in the army. You're in my Army." Unfortunately, Army soldiers make terrible shooters. I often ask players to stand at attention similar to the stance soldiers execute in the military. Then I ask if they are comfortable. "No way," is usually the response. So if it were so difficult to do, why would anyone shoot this way? Unfortunately this is just another "outdated" concept that coaches have been handing down from generation to generation.

There are virtually no great shooters that go straight up and down. If you check out all the great shooters in the NBA, the majority goes slightly backwards and only a few actually go forward as they shoot (examples include: Steve Kerr, Steve Nash and Danny Ferry).

Basketball coaches emphasize balance to their players. The problem is that most don't understand what true balance is all about or where it comes from. The one sport where an athlete is benefited by being straight up and down in a vertical position is bodybuilding. This is the only sport where having a great deal of tension actually helps the performer. As a shooter, however, it is impossible to go straight up and down. The back, neck and shoulders can't properly work in a vertical position. The pressure and tension becomes too great and the shot becomes similar to a spasm.

When the shot becomes a spasm, the player will start losing power/extension and usually fall short. I truly believe 90% of all short misses deal with players shooting up and down like a human popsicle stick. Unfortunately most coaches have no understanding regarding the shoulder region and ALWAYS seem to blame it on the legs ("Bend them more!"). You can bend them as much as you want, but the player will continue to miss short unless he fixes the shoulder and neck region.

I'M SOOOOOO TENSE

Where do you feel tension in your body? You've had a bad day at the office or at school. Where do you feel it? Your sister or brother has just thrown away your homework. You scream at them! You're tense. Where do you feel it? You don't feel it in your knees, your toes or your thighs.

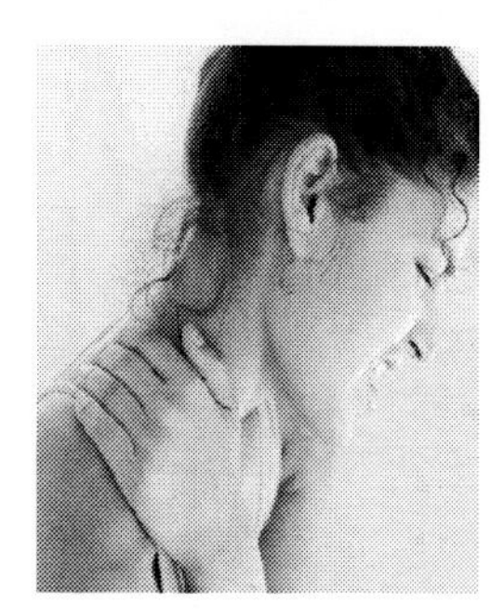

Tension can be found in two main areas—your hands and your neck/shoulder area. Imagine walking around all day tensing your shoulders and neck. With each step you take, you become the "Bug Man" from the motion picture, "Men in Black." How comfortable would this feel? Obviously no one wishes to walk in this tense manner. So if no one wants to be like the "Bug Man" then why do the majority of basketball players shoot like him?

A player can never be tense when shooting. The tenser a player, the more spastic the shot becomes. When I start working with a player, I will put my hands lightly on his shoulders and ask him to shoot the ball. I can feel how tense he is by the pressure onto my hands from his neck and shoulder region. Some players have so much tension there that we should put a lump of coal on their shoulders and if we come back in a week we would have two diamonds.

DON'T FIGHT IT

Most young players fight their shoulders, neck and body when shooting. The great shooters, on the other hand, relax their shoulders. At no point do they struggle with tension. If you watch a great shooter, the movements are effortless. If you watch a poor shooter, the shoulders, head and neck rarely work together.

SWAY DETAILS

The "Sway" is a very simple, but effective technique that will help the shoulders to relax while giving the shot additional arc. Please note that while this is a crucial element in accurate shooting, it is never mentioned by basketball coaches when teaching shooting. The players which use the sway are the best shooters year in and year out at the college and professional ranks. I truly believe this technique is a MUST for all players no matter what position that player plays.

When shooting, your feet should "sweep" or "sway" in front of your body. This will allow your shoulders to "sway" back. Because you will land equally on both feet, this is not considered a fade-away jump shot. A fade-away is when a player only lands on one foot.

When learning the Sway is it crucial to shoot many shots without the ball to get used to the feet forward and the shoulders back.

LOWER BODY SWAY

Lastly, it is crucial that a player focuses on keeping the feet narrow while swaying. Proper alignment starts with a narrow base. If you have a wide base, chances are you will become a two shoulder and two eyed shooter. The best shooters in the world are narrow shooters. The worst shooters are generally wide shooters. If you think back to all the worst shooters you have known, you probably will remember that each player was also a wide shooter. The wider a shooter becomes the more off balanced and slower that player becomes.

When landing it is essential that a player narrows his shooting base. When a player brings his feet closer together, the feet will naturally sweep. In other words, the feet will lead which forces to shoulders to trail. This will allow the shoulders to relax while shooting.

POWER WITH SWAY

There are two shooting aspects that will give a shot power: the Elbow (you will learn more about this in the next chapter) and the Sway. The premise of the sway is pretty simple, the further you move back, the more sway you use. When shooting from the three point line, you will sway only a few inches. It's a simple shot and you don't need much power here. With a three pointer you will need to sway six inches. I have many of my players from high school through professional levels that can shoot from 25-28 feet out simply because they understand that they receive additional power on their shot through the Sway.

TENSION AND PRESSURE

A large reason that a player should sway concerns how the human body is designed. It should be understood that each person has different shoulders and a neck region. Former Boston Celtic great, Kevin McHale, had naturally wide and awkward shoulders. Young players obviously don't have the same problems that muscle bound power forwards in the NBA have.

I have many students who have been told by their coaches that they should always shoot straight up and down. The true irony here is that if they don't sway they have little chance of making the shot, especially if they have wide shoulders.

Jared Sullinger, All-American from Ohio State is a player I have worked with. Jared has great hand eye coordination for his size (6'8"), but has wide shoulders. He has good release, but has been known to struggle with his shot at the free-throw line. The main reason is because of his shoulders. When he sways, he is an outstanding free-throw shooter. When he goes straight up and down, he struggles. It is really that simple.

Shooting should always be an easy motion. So then why do we make it so difficult? I can watch a pure shooter for hours. The form generally looks effortless as the entire body works in unity. Great shooters rarely tense their shoulder muscles. Poor shooters, on the other hand, tense their shoulders and neck muscles constantly.

I have followed "hoops" for well over 30 years, and I have NEVER heard the following words uttered by a basketball announcer: "Look at what a great shooter he is. He's got a nice hard shot!" Of course, I have heard this phrase (or close to it) thousands of times: "That player is a great shooter. He has a nice soft shot!" How effective your touch is greatly depends on how rigid and tense your shoulders become. If your shoulders are loose, often times your shot will be soft. If you shoulders are tense, chances are your shot will also be hard.

Lastly, I believe it is imperative for girls to adopt the Sway. Girls generally shoot more in an up and down motion than boys, but have less strength. Because of this, girls that constantly shoot up and down constantly struggle. I truly believe girls that have their shoulders back will play Division I basketball.

HUMMING FOR TENSION

To see how much pressure you possess in your shot, try this tip. Start at the top of the key and begin humming loud enough so you can hear yourself. Now bounce three times with your feet (similar to a kangaroo's bounce) and continue humming. After the third bounce shoot the ball at the basket. Only stop humming after you have released the ball. Did you hear your humming become louder at any point or did your voice crack? If you did hear this then it means you have tension in that part of your shot.

When a person's voice rises, it means they are becoming tenser. If you noticed that your humming stopped before your release occurred, then you stopped breathing, which will also force your body to become tense. As you bounce into your shot it is important to become relaxed and to have your humming in one tone. This is an effective drill as you will understand how much tension is in your body, especially your shoulders. This drill came from a teaching tool that golfers often do on their back swing to judge overall tension.

Of the five major parts of the jump shot, the shoulders and neck are easily the hardest aspect for most players to overcome. Because players are dealing with large upper body muscles that are prone to tension and strain, it can take as long as six months to a year to have the shoulders and neck at ease when shooting. For most shooters, this becomes the last shooting region to completely change.

THE CONSTIPATED SHOOTER

Similar to the shoulders, the neck and head are a huge component of accurate shooting. One of the biggest problems with younger players is what I have termed the "Constipated Shooter Syndrome." Often times when younger players shoot, their chin drops to their chest which forces the shoulders and neck to suddenly tense. It actually appears as if the player is constipated. I'll see players that weigh only 100 pounds suddenly having three chins because of their chin and head snapping down into the chest. As you watch them shooting, it is as if each player is having a whiplash forward. This is one of the biggest problems for younger players. If this "syndrome" is occurring when shooting, it must be corrected as soon as possible.

The way to correct it is simple to explain but can be difficult to perform. As the shoulders sway back, the head needs to follow. Throughout The Pro Shooting Secrets I have discussed the importance of the entire body working together. At no point should parts of the body be working separately especially the neck, head and shoulders. As the player shoots, the chin needs to rise for the shot to feel comfortable.

The best way to break this ugly habit is to measure the distance between the chin and the chest before shooting. For most players this will be 5-8 inches depending on how long their neck is. Then ask them to shoot and hold their follow-through for a longer period of time. Properly measure the neck after shooting and discover the distance. Often times the measurements can be 6 inches before and 1 inch after which means there is five inches of pure tension. The measurements before the player shoots and after must be nearly the same. The key for the shooter here is to get the same distance between chin and neck on every shot they attempt. If this is inconsistent, the shot's accuracy will generally be inconstant.

Another recommendation is to shoot into a mirror to clear up the "Constipated Shooter." A player may not have the luxury of a person to be measuring the distance between the chin and the chest on each and every shot. When the shooter can look into a mirror and see this distance for himself, it should help clear up the problem.

DON'T HANG YOURSELF!!!

"Do not go into the light."
JoBeth Williams as Diane Freeling
From the Motion Picture, "Poltergeist"

Another terrible problem with the neck and shoulders is the "Hanging Method." Coaches often instruct players that they should shoot high as if they were trying to shoot to the ceiling. Unfortunately, the basket is only 10 feet tall and not attached to the ceiling. When players attempt to shoot this high, the arms naturally rise and the shoulders and neck suddenly tense. In other words, they have created a human noose and are now hanging themselves. Obviously, hanging yourself and shooting don't mix very well.

The hanging method doesn't work, especially for younger players who lose obvious power when shooting in this uncomfortable style. To change this habit (and it needs to be changed), picture the shooting hole that you look through as a television set. When you watch TV, do you sit as close as you can and try to put your face into the glass? Obviously not, but that is what is occurring when you shoot. Imagine your shooting hole as a glaring television. You want to look at it, but never into it. Your shooting bicep should be right around the jaw line when taking a jump shot.

To correct the hanging method, make sure your shoulders and head are relaxed. Similar to the constipated shooter, the only way to break this terrible habit is to shoot into a mirror without a basketball.

SHOOT WITH YOUR ARMS

When you're shooting, make sure you don't use your neck to shoot. I have seen many poor shooters that come to me looking for accuracy, but have no chance of consistently making their shot because of tension from their neck. I can watch great shooters all day long, mainly because their form is so effortless. This effortless appearance is often because good shooters shoot with their arms and never do they tense their neck and shoulder muscles. When players shoot with their shoulders in a straight up and down motion, the neck muscles have a tendency of tightening.

CHAPTER 14 WRAP UP:

- The difference between an average shooter and a great shooter lies in the individual's shoulders and neck region.
- A player can't go straight up and down when shooting. The human body is not designed to go up and down.
- Tension can be found in two areas of a person—your hands and your neck/ shoulder area
- The tenser you become, the more spastic your shot will become.

SECTION IV:

ADDITIONAL SHOOTING ASPECTS

"You can practice shooting eight hours a day, but if your technique is wrong, then all you become is very good at shooting the wrong way."

Michael Jordan
Basketball Hall of Fame Player

15. ADDITIONAL COMPONENTS

I. THE STARTING POSITION & HOLD

If you hold the ball wrong, chances are that you will shoot the ball wrong. One of the most common problems for inaccurate shooters is the placement of the hand on the ball. The shooting hand should always be under the ball. When holding the ball, it will be similar to having two thumbs. The index finger should be placed in the middle with one thumb on one side, and the others three fingers becoming one thumb. If you place the middle finger in the middle of the ball, you will find the ball will often rotate to the side.

Because of a lack of strength, many younger players hold the ball not under, but more toward the top. This leads to a problem of consistency as they usually miss short. By placing your hand under the shot, your arch will dramatically increase.

Once again, it is necessary that the index finger is in the middle of the ball and the hold is under the ball. It cannot be on the side. By placing the hand on the side, the ball will rotate off the incorrect fingers and the shot will always miss to the side of the rim.

SHOOTING WRIST LOOSE

There should be no tension in the wrist. I have heard coaches tell their players to put so much tension and pressure on your wrist that wrinkles will appear. The problem with having wrinkles is that it becomes similar to a cocked motion much like a shot put. A shot putting motion is an explosive and violent toss. A shooting motion, on the other hand, is a pure and effortless act. Keep the wrist tension free and your shot will become much softer.

SHOOTING HAND FREE OF TENSION

When holding a ball, the hand needs to be relaxed. Too often I find many players hold the ball so tightly that it appears as if they are trying to strangle the ball. Remember, Spalding or Wilson is your friend that how you treat your friend by trying to suffocate it?

There are two true areas on a body that people generally feel the most tension the neck and shoulder region and in the hands. We will discuss the neck and shoulder region in a later chapter. Concerning the hands, it is vital that a shooter relaxes them when he shoots. If you hold the ball in a tense manner, your shot will naturally be tense, which will generally force you to miss your shot long.

Coaches put an incredible emphasis from a young age on protecting the ball. Because of this, players have a tendency to hold the ball tightly. I can understand holding onto the ball tightly if a defender is harassing you. This makes obvious sense as protecting the ball is crucial if you are trying to avoid a turnover. When you are open for a shot, however, you must hold the ball lightly with the shooting hand void of tension. Players often become worried that if they hold onto it in a loose manner when shooting that the ball will slip out of their hands. This will not happen because you will still have the "off hand" helping out and guiding the ball.

Again, remember a shooting hand should always be relaxed and free of tension and anxiety. Players who have a tendency of missing a great amount of shots that go in and out usually have a tight hold on the ball. A good rule of thumb is to hold the ball lightly when you're shooting and hold it tighter when a defender is closely guarding you.

THE STARTING POINT

Another one of the great misconceptions of the shot concerns where the ball actually starts. A mistaken belief by many coaches is that the higher the shot begins, the better it is because the shot cannot be blocked from this position. I've seen coaches teach their players to begin the shot above the head, only to later watch a game played by that team and see those players get their shot blocked continuously.

What coaches don't understand is that it is impossible to start the shot above the head every time and still be accurate. The most important component here that everyone fails to understand is the starting point is where the pass is actually caught. Most basketball passes are chest passes which means the pass is passed from the chest and is generally caught in the chest region. In other words, this is where the shot should begin. Why would you catch it at your chest, bring it up to your head, stop and then shoot it? The shot becomes slow and one that can easily be blocked.

When a player shoots off the dribble he will generally bring it up to his shot pocket which is also based around the chest as well. In other words, both the shot off the pass and the shot off the dribble starts at or near the shoulder region.

NO POWER, NO SHOT

When you begin your shot above your head, you will struggle not only with speed but also with your power. The higher you shoot, the less power and range a player usually has. If you watch a player that begins his shot above the eyes, usually the furthest out he will be able to shoot consistently is 10-12 feet. If you watch a guard that understands where his proper starting location is and how to use his elbow for overall power, you will then see a player with unlimited range.

Much of your shooting power comes from your elbow. The ball should start 3-6 inches from the chest. To understand the importance of this starting point I usually will pick out a player at a camp and ask him, "Let's say you have super human powers. You're Superman without the red cape, and you see a runaway bus coming toward a playground. You have to stop the bus, RIGHT? So how are you going to stop this bus?" I then give three options to choose from. "You can stop it with your arms fully stretched out OR with your elbow back and your hands 3-6 inches from your chest OR with your elbow far back and your hands directly next to your chest. Which one are you going to choose?" More than 50% of the time the players choose to stop the bus with their arms fully extended. "Show me how," I respond. They put their arms out in front of their chest and lock them. I come along and push on their arms, which forces the player to be off balance and stagger. "I'll visit you in the hospital," I respond. After we demonstrate all three different choices, the player quickly understands that there is truly only one option that offers balance and power—the elbow back and your hands being 3-6 inches from your chest. This is the area from which a player has the greatest natural shooting position strength. Players also need to start the shot near their chest so the defender can't strip it. The further they are away from their chest, the easier it is for the defender to touch.

The elbow, forearm and bicep need to be in a comfortable "V" position. The forearm needs to be directed at the basket. The most common shooting position taught today is the "L" shape. When you put your arm in an "L" position your forearm becomes directed at the ceiling, which forces the player to shoot straight up and lose power. The basket is not attached to the ceiling but is only 10 feet above the ground. The "V" position allows the player to shoot more accurately than the stiff and flawed "L" form.

II. THE ELBOW

The elbow is the least talked about shooting component, but is one of the most important. The elbow gives a shooter additional power. You have already read in a previous chapter that most coaches believe a player's power comes 100% from the legs. This is not completely accurate, however. Shooting with the "Sway" is important to gain extra power, but proper use of the elbow gives it extra boost of power.

In its simplest form, the elbow's mechanics are similar to a slingshot. Think about how uncomplicated a slingshot is. To get additional power on this primitive toy, you pull it back further. The same theory applies to the elbow in shooting. Few players know this shooting secret, however. The further you pull the elbow back, the more power the shooter receives and the further the shot will travel.

Like any thing good, the elbow can also be used in an incorrect manner. Imagine using a wooden slingshot and pulling it back as far as you can. Sooner or later the sling shot will break. The same concept can be said if you pull back the elbow too much. After a certain point, you lose your shot's power. Each person is different because of overall strength and body structure (length of arms) and therefore each player needs to experiment with the elbow to see what feels comfortable and for overall accuracy.

THE ELBOW MUST BE LOOSE

If the elbow is tight, your shot will naturally be tight. The elbow is similar to a door hinge. If the door hinge is loose, the door works perfect. If the hinge is rusty and tight, the door will not work as well. The elbow must be loose when shooting. You cannot get distance in your shot if you tense your elbow.

THE CATCH

From the first time a player ever steps foot onto a basketball court, he hears coaches scream, "Go meet the pass. Go get it!" That player therefore outstretches his arms to catch all passes. There's only one problem here. How does a player go meet the pass and then try to shoot the ball accurately? After all, by the time you outstretch your arms, catch it and then bring it to your starting position, the defender will probably be on you. So what do you do?

Catching a pass for a jump shot is similar to trying to hit a curve ball in baseball. If you don't know how to properly hit a curve, you will normally be impatient, swing before the ball gets to the plate and strike out. The common phrase that most baseball hitting coaches use is "Wait on the curve." By being patient and waiting on the curve ball, the batter allows himself enough time for the pitch to properly break. Once the pitch breaks, the ball is much easier to hit. When you are impatient and catch the ball with your arms extended, you loose your power and your entire form.

You should wait on the ball and let it come to you when you are open. If you're being tightly guarded, however, you will need to "go meet the pass." You should remember, however, that chances are good that you don't have an open shot anymore since the defender is that close. Before the ball is even passed you need to ask yourself the question, "If the ball is passed to me right now, am I open or is the defender too close to me to get an open shot?" If you're open, be patient and let the ball come to you. You should catch the ball anywhere from 3-6 inches from your chest. If you're being guarded, reach out and go get the ball.

When a player catches the ball in his pocket it is crucial that the he does not bring the ball down. If this happens, the shot will take longer and the defender will have an opportunity to either block the shot. If the pass is decent, the shooter can bring his elbow back but can never bring the ball down. The lowest the ball should ever dip (unless it's a low pass) when attempting a shot is the shoulder region.

If the pass is near the head region, the shooter will have to bring it down in the shooting pocket. Because of the Hop (you will read about that when you get to the LOWER BODY section), the shooter will have enough time to get this shot off if he brings it to his starting point (the shooting pocket). Unless you are shooting from within ten feet, you do not have the proper strength to catch the pass at or above the head level. Lastly, concerning how to catch a pass, please make sure you are ready to shoot once the ball comes to you. I see players all the time catch a pass with both elbows pointed outward. By the time they catch the pass and rotate their hands so they are ready to shoot, the defender can easily guard them. If you're open for a shot, catch the ball like you're ready to shoot it. If you're being guarded, catch the ball in a protected position with both elbows out. Please note that the player must know which way he needs to properly catch the pass before it is actually thrown.

THE HITCH

A "Hitch" is anytime the ball goes above or behind a player's head while shooting. Often when the ball is brought back behind the head, the motion can turn into a throwing motion. In short, this action becomes similar to a catapulting motion.

The reason for having the hitch usually revolves around how the player catches the pass. I guarantee that this type of player catches the ball by going out and meeting the ball. Once you have your arms fully extended, your ability to shoot the ball is greatly impaired. At this point you have two choices: to bring the ball back into your shooting pocket, which will take a great deal of time, or bring the ball back to your head in a catapult motion.

If you shoot with a hitch, you must understand that your biggest problem will be constantly falling short on your shot. Because the hitch motion will force you to push the ball out, it is crucial to properly use your shoulders and fade slightly. You will read about the shoulders in much greater detail in an upcoming chapter. By fading with the hitch, the ball has a tendency of arching more, thus preventing the shot from missing short.

Please understand that if you do start your shot a foot or more out in front of you, chances become much greater that a player will be able to strip it (especially those pesky small guards with quick hands). If you watch any pure shooter, that player will start his shot with the ball tucked near his body.

III. THE OFF HAND

A player's off hand (the non-shooting hand) is a crucial part of shooting with accuracy. The off hand serves as a guide for the shot, but more importantly, it helps to balance the entire body. If you want to see if a player is a good shooter, simply watch his off hand. Players that pull their off hand away or down while shooting are prone to struggle.

The off hand can be easy to correct if the player is open minded. It usually takes only a few minutes to change and the shooter should also feel comfortable while making this change after the first five minutes.

Players may demonstrate a variety of poor off hand mechanics from pulling it to the side or down (this causes the player to be off balanced) or pulling it above the shooting hand (which forces the player to tense). Improper use of the off hand can affect shooting accuracy by as much as 30-40% for younger players because of a lack of strength and coordination.

"JAMAAL TAYLOR AND THE OFF HAND"

In spring of 1998, Larry Taylor called me requesting a shooting session for his 15 year old son, Jamaal. Jamaal, who just concluded his sophomore season on the Junior Varsity team at Canyon High School, had never made a three point shot in game competition and desperately needed shooting assistance.

The first time he came to a session, I discovered that Jamaal's problem area was clearly his off hand (his left). He would shoot the ball with his right hand and immediately pull his left hand away as if it was shot from cannon. Because his left hand pulled so badly, his body was off balanced forcing his shooting hand to pull to the right. In fact, he looked similar to a breaststroke swimmer. Jamaal's off hand was decimating his overall shooting accuracy. I immediately instructed him to finish his shot with his left hand 5-6 inches from his right. But Jamaal's muscle memory was so poor that his left hand continued to flail. Finally I said, "Jamaal, try to shoot and pull your off hand over and lightly touch it to your right." I was willing to try anything to get his shot to become more balanced. To my surprise Jamaal made a shot, and another and another. Within five minutes he would get the off hand technique completely down.

Jamaal drastically improved his shooting form and accuracy throughout the next two years. He shattered all three point school records at Canyon High School. My experience with Jamaal also caused me to modify my philosophy concerning the off hand. Within weeks, I transformed all of my shooters to touch the off hand with the release. I saw drastic improvements with this new technique, especially from players who had been struggling with their upper body balance.

IT'S ABOUT BALANCE

As previously mentioned, the off hand is used as a balancing agent. In fact, you get a majority of your balance from your legs, feet and the off hand. This is very similar to a diver. You will never see a championship diver entering the water with his arms flying. Shooting needs to be looked at in the same manner. It should be remembered that a human arm and hand weighs about five pounds. When you pull your off hand completely from your shot, it's as if you are trying to shoot with one hand and trying to lift a five pound dumbbell with the other hand. In other words, when the off hand pulls away it becomes much more difficult to shoot with accuracy because you will always be slightly off balanced.

Balance is crucial in shooting. Reggie Miller had one of the most unique shots in all of basketball. He shot by crossing his left hand over his right. Miller did this so he could achieve total balance. My guess is that when he was growing up in Riverside, California, Reggie played a lot of pickup ball with his older brother Darrell (would later professional baseball) and sister Cheryl (considered one of the greatest women's players of all time) and would get thrown around a lot. Soon he discovered you have a lot more balance if you cross your hands than threw your hands apart.

While the Pro Shot System does not want to cross the hands as radically as Miller did, our off hand concept of touching is very similar.

IT'S ABOUT DOING THE SAME SHOT OVER AND OVER

When you touch your off hand with your shooting hand you receive not only balance but also a perfect guide. When your off hand wildly pulls down or away, chances are your release hand will also pull away. By bringing your shot together, you will perform the identical shot each time.

The off hand is similar to the Monorail track at Disneyland as it acts as a guide. If the track fails to properly work at this theme park, the Monorail will crash, people will die, and it will no longer be "The Happiest Place on Earth." By using the off hand in the same manner, it forces the shooting hand to stay straight.

Many of my students become cautious when I tell them to lightly touch their off hand to their shooting hand. It appears lightly touch their off hand to their shooting hand. It appears will instantly ignite and blow up. Please understand that it is perfectly fine to bring the shot together and touch. As long as you don't grab your shooting hand with your off hand or slap it, then it actually becomes beneficial to touch.

A shooter needs to resemble a diver much more than a breaststroke swimmer for overall balance. If the arms are constantly flailing, the shooter will be off balanced. Young shooters must focus on the off hand and touch it to the shooting hand because of their overall lack of strength.

DON'T SHOOT WITH TWO HANDS

Players should only shoot with one hand. Over a half a century ago, basketball players were instructed to shoot with two hands. The belief at that time was that if your left hand went to the left and your right hand went to the right, the ball would somehow stay straight. Obviously, this concept is frowned upon by today's coaches.

The Pro Shot Shooting System's off hand theory also helps players not to shoot with two hands. Obviously if the off hand pulls off you have a much better chance of turning the wrist out. This will force the player to shoot with two hands. If you have a problem shooting with two hands, it becomes crucial that you focus on touching the off hand to the shooting hand.

THE UNCONTROLABLE OFF HAND

You must have control of your off hand. One effective way to train the off hand to touch the right is the "feel" method. Most players rarely ever feel any part of their shot. When doing it correctly, it acts as a focus point for balance. Touching it will help as a guide, but it will also assist the muscle memory for overall balance while repeating the same shot time after time.

The pictures below clearly illustrate the difference between an off hand flying from the shot and one that is working with the release and is in total control. I was introduced to this player, Jeff, in late December 2004. I noticed immediately his off hand pulled from his shot. If you closely look at figure 1 it appears as if he is trying to "punch out" a teammate with his off hand. "Give me 10 minutes and I will change the whole structure of your shot by simply changing your off hand," I explained to him. Ten minutes later I took the second picture which illustrates a more balanced shooter.

"THE STRANGE BUT TRUE ALIEN HAND DISORDER"

A few years ago I was watching the television program, "20/20" about a brain disorder called the "Alien Hand." This inflicts people that can feel sensation in their hand, but believe that it is not part of their body, and they therefore have no control over its movements. In other words, a person could be making a peanut butter and jelly sandwich with one hand and the opposite hand can take the knife and try to stab that individual. Hollywood adapted a movie based around this disorder called "Idle Hands." I tell my students about the "Alien Hand" and ask them if they are afflicted with this rare disorder. They usually laugh and say, "No way." I then remind them that their shot appears as if "the off hand has been overcome by the Alien Hand."

THE TRAINING WHEEL

The Off Hand Touch is similar to a training wheel on a bike. The training wheel is an aid you use when learning to ride a bike. The Off hand touch is also an aid as it is used so young players have shooting balance. It is VERY important for players to touch from 3rd grade through middle school because of strength. Once the player gets to high school and no longer pulls away, he does not need to touch no longer, but keep the off hand next to the shooting hand. Many of our high school and collegiate players, however, still continue to touch because they feel comfortable with this technique.

CHAPTER 15 WRAP UP:

- The shooting hand should always be under the ball.
- It is necessary that the index finger is in the middle of the ball.
- There should be no tension in the wrist.
- Both the shot off the pass and the shot off the dribble starts at or near the shoulder region.
- The ball should start 3-6 inches from the chest.
- The elbow gives a shooter additional power.
- The elbow must be loose when shooting.
- A player's off hand (the opposite of the release) serves as a guide for the shooting, but more importantly it helps balance the entire body.
- You get a majority of your balance from your legs, feet and your off hand.
- When you touch your off hand with your shooting hand you receive not only balance, but also a perfect guide.

16. FIGURING OUT MISSES & AND CORRECTING ERRORS

Everyone misses shots because no basketball player will ever be perfect. Missing is simply a part of the game. In fact, the best players in the world miss half of the shots they attempt in games. The most important aspect a player can understand in correcting his errors is to ask himself, "What direction am I missing and how can I then correct these errors?"

I've seen players shoot in a practice or game and miss their shots the same way every time. They will shoot ten shots and miss all their shots short and will fail to adjust their shooting. They will just keep shooting and missing.

Great shooters rarely miss the same shot twice. They understand how they are missing and then will correct their shooting form appropriately. Poor players, on the other hand, usually don't realize how they are missing. I will watch a player miss over and over again short. Finally I'll ask him, "How are you missing? What direction—short, long, left or right?" Often times that player will not have an answer. Many players will actually answer incorrectly and say, "Long."

Sean Jackson is one of the smartest players I have ever coached. In only six months that he worked with me, Sean went from being an average college shooter to one of the most prolific three point shooters in all of NCAA men's basketball. His shooting philosophy is simple but very functional. I remember talking to him one afternoon when he said, "**I may miss two shots in a row, but I will never miss the same shot twice.** If I miss long on one shot, the next shot I will correct myself. I will refuse to miss long." If more players adopted Sean's philosophy about missing, there would definitely be more accurate shooters in this world.

It is crucial to fully understand the direction that you miss as well. Great shooters miss to the sides and rarely miss long. If Steve Nash shoots 100 shots in practice, chances are he will miss 2-3 shots to the side. On a good day he may not miss any shots to the sides. A poor shooter, on the other hand, will miss 60-70 shots to the side. We will discuss the importance of keeping your shot straight later in this chapter.

"THE INDELIBLE IMAGE"

Michael Jordan's last shot he ever took in a Chicago Bulls uniform would become his most famous shot in his NBA career. On June 14, 1998, Jordan hit a game winning twenty footer against the Utah Jazz. It gave the Bulls an 87-86 victory and their sixth championship in eight years.

Jordan would hold his follow-through on that shot for what seemed an eternity. Throughout the basketball world it became known as "The Pose." Afterwards the media asked him, "Why did you hold your shot for so long? Were you posing for the cameras because that might be the last shot you take in a Chicago Bulls uniform?" MJ, however, insisted it was not that at all. His jump shot had been falling short for most of the game and in the most important shot in his career, he made sure he would not fall short by extending his follow-through. Dave Kindred of the Sporting News writes, "It's fitting Jordan would leave an indelible image of such conquest. It's

The Last Shot, the dagger to Utah's heart, Jordan standing stock-still, his right arm held high, the hand just so. He insisted it was no pose. He said he'd been tired; his jump shot had been short, and this one he wanted done correctly. He called the exaggerated follow-through evidence of craft, not ego." That's why Jordan was so great.

Only great shooters truly can comprehend Jordan's mental approach. If you are struggling with your shot, you must fix it. Poor shooters have little understanding of this mindset. They will continue to miss over and over and fail to make the needed corrections. When I am working with a player and this occurs, I will finally stop and explain, "Imagine taking a math test. It's five questions and you miss the last question. The next week you miss the same question. The same question continues to appear on each test and you continue to miss it week after week. Your grade in the class is beginning to suffer because of it. What are you going to do? The logical answer would be that you correct the problem. The problem is that most poor shooters don't look upon athletics like academics. If they did, they would figure out why they miss and become much more productive shooters."

ELIMINATE YOUR MISSES

In shooting, you need to figure out how you are missing. Are your shots missing long, short, left or right? Once you understand the direction that you're missing, then you have to understand how to properly fix your shot. Most poor shooters fail to do both. Most great shooters, however, understand shooting is like a science experiment of collecting data and then discovering the answer.

There are four directions a shooter can miss—short, long, left, or right. As we have mentioned before, good shooters generally only miss straight (short or long). Poor shooters, however, will miss all four ways and can actually miss two ways at the same time. It is not uncommon to see a poor shooter miss long and to the right, or short and to the left.

I will often ask newer players that I'm working with if they know how to correct their shot when they miss. Most players shrug their shoulders. My question is, if you have something broken and you don't know how to repair it, how will you ever make it work properly? Anytime you miss, you must give your brain feedback as how to fix it.

Please look at the following ways to miss and ways to correct your shot. This table will greatly assist each shooter and should be used as a constant reference guide when the shot is just not falling.

GUIDE TO SHOOTING PERFECTION

MISSING TO THE SIDE (LEFT OR RIGHT) –

This is the most common way to miss (42%). This is also the easiest direction to correct, however. Please remember that quality shooters miss rarely to the sides. For the most part, they miss usually only short and long. Missing to the right or left is usually due to:

- Coming off the wrong finger(s). Usually this is attributed to the ball being dominated by the ring finger and the pinkie. The shooter needs to focus more on the ball coming off the index finger.
- The shooting release or shooting arm is pulling to the side. The shot must stay straight which means the finger and the arm must be straight.
- The shooter is fading to the side. This usually occurs only with older players. It should be remembered that while it is fine to use the fade away to fade backwards, fading to the side usually does more damage than good.

MISSING SHORT—

This is one of most common ways to miss in all of shooting (40%). Missing short is usually due to:

- Being tense in your shoulders and neck. Obviously if you are tense in this area, you will be tense in your shot and it will usually fall short
- Being lazy with your release and releasing too low. You need to release higher.
- Lack of power. This usually occurs when the elbow comes out on the shot. It should be remembered that the elbow is the primary power source for shooting.

MISSING LONG—

This is the rarest of the misses at 18%. This is most common with the muscle bound players. Missing long is usually due to:

- Trying too hard to make the shot. This occurs when the shooter uses too much power and force.
- Being tense in your shoulders, neck and hands. When you're tense, your muscles can contract giving you limited power, or they can contract giving you a seizure like shot and making you actually throw the shot.

GAME MISSES

A player should never stop shooting in a game no matter how poorly that individual is missing. Instead of shutting it down, get your information process similar to what Jordan did against the Jazz. Ask yourself, "How am I missing?" When you come up with the proper answer then follow it up by asking yourself, "What part of my body is making me miss?" An example would be that you know you're missing short on your shot. You ask yourself, "Is my follow-through high enough?" It feels like it and looks like it (the finger is above the rim). It can't be the release. You move on. "Are my head and shoulders tense?" Normally a player knows instantly if they are tense or not. You believe there is little if no tension. "Am I losing power on my shot?" You feel a little fatigued and decide that this is the correct answer. On your next shot you use more elbow and you swish your next three point shot.

This deduction and analysis must begin in practice. Once you feel comfortable and understand shooting disciplines, you will soon begin using it in games. Sometimes, however, even the best shooters get so wrapped up in the emotions of a game that they temporarily forget how to adjust their shot. Because basketball is such a fast pace game, it can be very easy to do.

SMILE AND KEEP SHOOTING

"Why you smiling like that?"
Gimbel's Manager
"Because I like smiling. Smiling's my favorite."
Will Farrell as Buddy the Elf
From the motion picture, "Elf"

Shooting is a delicate art form. I often look at a shooter as a precious piece of art that can make you a fortune or can shatter to the point that all you have is a worthless pile of garbage. I once had a high school shooter, Alex Landa, start missing in a game. During a timeout he stared at his shooting hand as if it had a mind of its own. "Thou have forsaken me." I ordered him into our nearby locker room to shoot 50 shots against the wall. He returned a few minutes later to make three consecutive three pointers which helped to lead us to victory.

The best advice for players when they are mired in a mini shooting slump is to refocus on the finger, figure out why they're missing, and refuse to miss that way again. Then take a deep breath and smile. I see players shooting poorly and their faces usually tell the whole story. If a player has a look of frustration written on his face, he normally is playing and shooting poorly. If a player is smiling, he is usually playing and shooting well. In other words, how you look is usually how you're playing.

CHAPTER 16 WRAP UP:

- The most important aspect a player can understand is how they miss and how to correct the errors.
- Great players will rarely miss the same shot twice. They understand how they miss and will correct their shooting form.
- In shooting, you first need to figure out the direction that you are missing.
- Once you understand the direction that you're missing, then you have to understand how to properly fix it.

17. FREE THROW SHOOTING

"We're shooting 100 percent - 60 percent from the field and 40 percent from the free throw line."
Norm Stewart
Former Missouri Head Basketball Coach

The free throw is the easiest shot in basketball because the rim never moves. What's more, you will always stand 13' 9" to the dead center of the rim and 15' to the backboard. You also have nearly 10 seconds to shoot the ball and no one can ever contest it. Simple, huh? Tell that to Shaquille O'Neal, Ben Wallace and yes, even Tim Duncan. They all shoot barely 50% lifetime in their NBA careers from the charity stripe.

Shaquille is the most world-renowned poor free throw shooter since Wilt Chamberlain. In the 2004 NBA Playoffs, Shaq shot a woeful 49% for the Lakers. This performance led Barry, considered one of the best free throw Rick shooters of all-time, to proclaim in the San Francisco Herald Examiner, "SHAQUILLE O'NEAL IS, without debate, the most dominant center in today's NBA. At 7-foot-1 and 340 pounds, his size alone allows him to do things that other centers only dream about. He is a mix of power, athleticism, and finesse. But all of this cannot make up for the fact that he is a horrible free throw shooter. Did I say horrible? How about horrendous, dreadful, atrocious and appalling too?" Come on Rick—don't pick on Shaq like that. What he should also be doing picking on 100 other players currently in the NBA. Free throw shooting has definitely become a lost art form. In today's highflying acrobatic circus we call basketball, players have forgotten the importance of the simple free throw shot. The name actually tells how easy it should be. It's a FREE throw. In other words—a free shot.

FREE THROW SHOOTING IS IMPORTANT!

"When the other factors are equal (team movement, quickness, size, and outstanding coaching), the teams who shoot free throws well and have a couple good outside shooters are almost always the ones who win championships."
Tom Norland
Shooting Coach

Free throw shooting wins the close games. Free throw shooting wins championships. When I watch March Madness each year I'm amazed at how many games are actually decided at the line in the last two minutes. If you want to win anything worthwhile, chances are that team will have to prove it at the free throw line. In the 2003 NCAA Championship Game, Kansas only made 12 out of 30 free throws and narrowly lost to Syracuse, 81-78. Coach Roy Williams must still constantly think to himself, "We were so close. If we could have just made our free throws."

No one wants to lose championships and close games either. But it will happen if the better players on a team are poor free throw shooters. Similar to proper shooting, players have to always be trying to work on their free throw technique and improve their skills from the line. Good free throw shooting takes countless hours of practice to master the mental and physical skills. As you read on you'll discover that I will break the free throw down into minute details. Please understand that when all is said and done, it still does come down to the shooter's technique. Shaquille O'Neal does practice his free throws. For quite awhile he had a key to the Manhattan Beach Middle School gym and would go there late at night to practice his shooting. There's only one problem—Shaq has flawed technique. No matter how much he practices, he will still continue to miss.

"FOCUSING & CONCENTRATING INTO THE RECORD BOOKS"

The greatest free throw shooter in history is Dr. Tom Amberry. If you search his name in the NBA record books you will never locate it. If you get out the Guinness Book of World Records, however, you will discover that the fine Doctor made 2,750 free throws without a miss on November 15, 1993. That's an amazing feat, but more remarkable when one realizes that Dr. Tom accomplished this record at age 71.

Dr. Tom had retired from podiatry a few years before and had grown bored around the house. He needed an escape and found it with free throw shooting. A former collegiate player at University of North Dakota, Dr. Tom decided to pick up the basketball once again. At first he struggled to make ten shots consecutively. Each day he would go to the Rossmoor Center and spend 2-3 hours shooting free throws. Little did anyone realize the white haired gentleman on the far court would in time become the world's greatest free-throw shooter.

I have known Dr. Tom for nearly a decade. When we see each other we stop and talk about various free throw shooting concepts. In 1997 he gave me his book, "Free Throw—7 Steps to Success at the Free Throw Line." The book clearly explains the mental and physical side of accurate free throw shooting. Dr Tom's two main words that he uses when he speaks on free throw shooting are, "Focus and Concentration." He believes once a player gets their seven steps down, it comes down to how well that shooter focuses and concentrates at the line.

LOVE THAT LINE!

"About 75% of close games are won or lost at the free throw line."
Rick Mount
Former Purdue University All-American

If you want to be a great free throw shooter, you can never have a phobia at the line. You must have a strong desire to get there and once you are there, you have to be comfortable. When some players get fouled and approach the line they think, "No problem. This is an easy two points." Other players, like Shaq, who are known to struggle from the line will think, "I hate this. I don't want to be here." And of course their results can be disastrous. What a player thinks about when he is at the free throw line, he generally becomes. If he has excellent technique, practices a good amount of time at the line and enjoys being at the charity stripe, he will become a great free throw shooter. If he has poor technique, doesn't practice the shot often and hates stepping up to the line, he will always be a poor free throw shooter.

CONSUMED TO BE THE BEST FROM THE LINE

Thankfully, there are some players that want to become great free throw shooters and fully understand the work ethic it takes to become one. Steve Alford, current University of New Mexico Head Men's Head Coach, is one of the greatest free throw shooters in NCAA history. As a freshman at Indiana University, Alford led the entire nation in free throw shooting at 91.3%. In his four years at Indiana, he successfully connected on 90% of his free throws and is currently the fourth all-time career percentage leader in NCAA history. These feats did not take place by Alford deciding in college that he wanted to be a good free throw shooter, however. During his high school years, Alford was consumed with becoming an excellent free throw shooter. He would shoot 100 free throws a day and would always record the results. He then posted these shooting sheets throughout his bedroom. He knew exactly what he shot for a certain day, week or month. Alford was consumed with being the best at shooting free throws.

"I LIKE TO SHOOT FREE THROWS!"

Dylan Rigdon is the greatest free throw shooter I have ever coached. In the fall of 1985, I met Dylan in the halls of Mater Dei High School in Santa Ana, California. I had just been hired on the coaching staff and the lanky Dylan, then only a freshman, came up to me and remarked, "I like to shoot free throws." Not, 'Hi, nice to meet you,' or 'Welcome to Mater Dei." I didn't know how to respond to his remark. It was such an odd one coming from a 14 year old. "That's good," I responded.

Dylan practiced his free throw shooting on a daily basis. He would have to make a hundred each day before he called it quits. As a high school senior, Dylan led Orange County in free throw percentage. He would later take his shooting talents to nearby UC Irvine where he led the Big West Conference in free throw shooting percentage as a freshman. After his sophomore year at Irvine, he decided to go for bigger waters and transferred to University of Arizona.

In January, 2001, Arizona Head Coach Lute Olson's wife, Bobbi, succumbed to cancer and passed away. Dylan along with other former Arizona players went back for the funeral and stayed with Coach Olson. One night the players were talking about all the U of A records and how great of players each of them were in their college days. Dylan didn't say much. He was the sixth man on a team that went to the Final Four his senior season. Unfortunately, he had terrible timing as he happened to be at U of A at the same time as two exceptional guards: Damon Stoudamire and Khalid Reaves (runner-up in College of the Year balloting in 92-93 season). Both would become NBA lottery picks. One of Dylan's former teammates started to razz him about his role-playing career. Finally Coach Olson chimed in, "I bet you guys don't know this. Dylan holds more U of A records than any player in history—three." The room suddenly turned silent. The surfer boy from Laguna Beach with the pure jumper and the even purer free throw delivery, held three Arizona marks. Of course all three are free throwing records which include highest free throw career percentage (87%), seasonal percentage (89%) and most consecutive free throws without a miss (29). But records are records.

STEP 1:
FIND THE DOT AND SHOOT THE SAME WAY

How many times do you dribble? Do you always breathe the same way? Are you focused on one image EVERYTIME? A quality free throw shooter does the same repetitive motions on every shot. Sometimes they may even have quirky gestures in a part of their shot. Jeff Hornacek would scratch his face EVERTYTIME with his shooting hand. John Stockton would make gestures to his wife and kids EVERYTIME. Adrian Dantley would cradle the ball EVERYTIME.

The most important thing to remember here is that proper free throw shooting is muscle memory through repetition. If you change your release or how you dribble into the free throw each time, you will not have repetitive success from the line. The first thing you should do as you approach the line is to find the center of the free throw line. When gyms floors are being designed, painters will generally put a dot or a nail in the middle of the free throw line. When you find this center point, you should line up your shooting foot next to it. I've heard coaches tell their players to stand in the middle of the nail or dot. Actually, if a shooter does this, he is now 3-4 inches off center. A player shoots from his side (a right hander, for example, would shoot from the right side of his body) and not directly from the middle of his chest. The nail or dot is an excellent way to finding the center of the key as long as the player understands the shooting foot must line up with it.

Once you receive the ball from the referee, you must take the same amount of dribbles on each free throw attempt. You have to have consistency and this dribble sequence is really no different. There is no right or wrong answer when it comes to how many times you should dribble at the line. Dr. Tom Amberry takes three and encourages his students to do the same. I have seen other effective shooters take the ball from the referee and not use a dribble. Former NBA great Dennis Johnson added a dribble for each year he was in the NBA, which worked out perfectly in his first few seasons. The problem was that DJ played 14 years in the NBA which made each free throw opportunity seem like an eternity.

Please note that while there is no set dribble amount for accurate free throw shooting, there is a time limit. The rule is that once the ball is handed to the shooter, he must complete the shot before ten seconds. I have only seen this violation called a handful of times.

Staring at the rim also does not help you at the line. I've heard coaches yell to their players, "Concentrate!" and the free throw shooter stares so intently at the rim that I'm surprised it doesn't melt. In the opening scene of "Raiders of the Lost Ark", Indiana Jones' Peruvian guide stares at a beautiful idol with a wide-eyed and awestruck expression. Many times I attend games and see this same mystified look as the free throw shooter glares at the rim. It is as if they believe the rim is going to change colors or suddenly move.

I hate miniature golf because of schoolhouses and castles whose doors open and automatically close. Rarely do I get my putt into the large hole without hitting the shutting door at least two or three times. It's frustrating to worry about a moving target. But shooting a free throw does not have moving objects. The rim always stays the same. So why do so many players stare at the rim? This usually occurs because the shooter believes the word "concentrate" has a connotation of staring at an object until his eyes water or he passes out. If you stare at something for a long period of time, the object can literally change its size right before you. Your eyes can easily play tricks on you by staring at the rim as you dribble. That basketball goal starts becoming narrower and narrower until a small pea can't drop in it, let alone a full size basketball. For this reason, I have my players avoid eye contact with the rim until Step #2.

Lastly, concerning dribbling at the line, don't dribble the ball way out in front of you. The dribbles should be on your side and straight down as you prepare for Step #2. If you dribble well out in front of your body, you may attempt to try shooting from this unnatural position, which will force you to lose needed power

STEP 2:
PAUSE WITH THE ELBOW, BREATHE AND FOCUS

After taking your dribbles (the same amount every time), you need to effectively pause your shot into your shooting pocket. This is a middle portion of the free throw that is crucial for focusing and relaxing. When the free throw shooter pauses, he finally should look at the rim. Two things need to come together here.

The first is a breathing pattern. If you watch a poor free throw shooter at the line, chances are he will not have proper breathing techniques. Obviously, if the shooter fails to breathe, muscles will become tight and the shot will become tense. If you watch the top free throw shooters, most have the same breathing techniques once they pick up their dribble. Clearly visible to the television camera, it is generally a breath in and a breath out.

The second area that is crucial in Step 2 is having the right focus. Shooting a free throw is similar to shooting a jump shot when speaking of proper focusing. Don't think about the rim or the ball, but instead focus on you. As you pick up your dribble, your focus should turn to one thought—finger through the rim. You should never turn your attention to the fat lady in the stands, the peanut vender with the nasal voice, the score, your parents, your coach, or your entire shot. The idea of "making it" is never a thought in your mind. Remember the problem that Karl Malone had when he was a rookie with having too many thoughts in his head. Clear your mind, take that breath and focus on your release and that magical finger.

Dr. Tom Amberry focuses his free throw by imagining his arm as being 15 feet long. Other shooting coaches instruct to not think of anything when shooting a free throw. This is very risky. There's a voice inside a brain that's called 'The Little Voice." This is the one that is constantly giving a person feedback. Often times this voice can have a negative tone. This is the voice that you hear when you approach the free throw line as it starts saying, "Don't miss. You better make it." Other times it gives pressurized feedback that may include such phrases as, "Get arch on your shot," or you better extend." By not thinking of a thought or an idea, you are taking a big chance that the "Little Voice" will come to your free throw party and completely wreck it.

If you focus on only one thought or idea every time, however, your chances of free throwing success rapidly increases. One preconceived thought will not allow any other beliefs in. If you think to yourself, "Finger through the rim" throughout Step 2, you will not hear anything from "The Little Voice" that will further confuse you. The "Voice" cannot overcome a solid and constant demand and therefore everything else will become muted out.

Don't stare at the rim. While orange is a bright and pretty color, it's not worthy of staring at it. Similar to jump shooting, don't focus on the front or back of the rim. I've noticed that the players that most often focus on the front of the rim usually miss short and the players that concentrate on the back of the rim can often be found missing long. It makes sense to look at the entire rim.

"A HALL OF FAME PERFORMER"

Of all the students I have coached, Bonnie Samuelson is the only one that is enshrined in the Basketball Hall of Fame. Bonnie did the impossible as she won the Lions United States Free throw Championship in back to back years (2004 and 2005). For her accomplishments Bonnie's name will forever be enshrined in the Hall.

If you ask Bonnie (who would later play for Stanford University) .why she is such a great free throw shooter she will smile and say it's just focus and a lot of practice. Her father, Jon, a former high school and collegiate standout at Chapman University, explains the focus part. "Bonnie's concentration at the line is truly amazing. I actually believe she could be shooting at one end, a part of the roof could collapse at the other end, and she wouldn't notice. She would keep on shooting."

STEP 3:
THE RELEASE

Once again we need to be focused as we enter the release. If you allow your mind to be totally free, you will find your shot will be inconsistent and generally will be all over the place. If you allow yourself to be focused and disciplined, you will become one of the best free throw shooters on your team and in your league.

Focusing on your shot is huge, but proper repetition comes into play once again as you shoot. Dr. Tom Amberry is the greatest free thrower ever. His record speaks for itself. Dr. Amberry, however, also has an ugly shooting release. Dr. Amberry shoots the free throw and snaps his arm back after his release. If one of my students did this, I would find the closest pool and throw him in it.

Dr. Tom's theories make perfect sense. If you watch poor shooters, they never focus and they usually never shoot the same shot twice in a row. The best free throw shooters, on the other hand, always use the amount of dribbles, always take the same type of breaths, always have the same focus and lastly, always release the same. In other words, it's perfect repetition.

Every shooter should have a perfect follow-through. While Dr. Amberry has been successful with his release, I do not suggest everyone should try that at home. Perfect shooting often is about releasing the ball in a flawless manner and free throw shooting is really no different.

STEP 4:
BELIEVE

As mentioned earlier in this chapter, you have to want to get to the free throw line and you have to believe in your shooting abilities. If your technique is poor then you must be open to change. When you close your mind to all changes, you basically sit in the dark. I have a saying I tell my students: "When you stop believing, you're dead. When you stop learning, you're dead. Always believe and learn."

"THE BEETHOVEN OF THE STRIPE FALLS ON DEAF EARS"

One evening in July, 2004, I ran into Dr. Tom Amberry and started talking to him for an hour on how to properly educate students in free throw shooting. Dr. Amberry had successfully served as a part-time shooting coach to the Chicago Bulls earlier that year and had been back in Southern California for only a few months.

"Not all kids want to learn," Dr Tom explained. He told me a story about a high school player from Chicago. A decent athlete, this player was a terrible free throw shooter. Realizing he needed assistance at the line, his parents contacted Dr. Tom to work with him in Southern California. The family flew out for six days, stayed in a nearby hotel, rented a car to get around, paid the gym rental fee and also paid Dr. Tom to privately work with their son. In total, the expenses were well over $5,000. "And the amazing part about this was that the kid didn't want to be there. He refused to listen to me and because of this, he never really improved

I found the story astonishing and almost impossible to believe. Here the player was spending his family's hard earned money, and he's being coached by the greatest free throw shooter in the world and he basically didn't wish to listen. It would be similar to taking piano lessons from Beethoven. How could he not listen? The 30% free throw shooter flew back to Chicago as a 30% free throw shooter because he refused to listen and learn.

SHAQ vs. BECKY

One area that I have yet to discuss concerning accurate free throw shooting is where your shot should actually begin once you stop dribbling. I have seen youth coaches teach their players to begin the shot above their head. The results are disastrous for the players as most of them either air ball or miss short. When you start a shot above your head, you lose your power. Shaquille O'Neal is one of the strongest NBA players of all time. He weighs 350 pounds (that's a conservative estimate) and yet he does not have enough power to properly shoot because he starts his free throw above his head. If you watch Shaq's shot closely, you will notice he starts fairly fluid, but then loses his strength. Instead of continuing to shoot toward and above the basket, he pushes out. Because of this pushing motion, his shots usually have limited arch and often fall short.

If Shaq doesn't have the strength to properly shoot a free throw from above his head, how will little twelve-year-old Becky find the needed power? Obviously, she won't. The question that I ask coaches teaching free throw shooting is: "Have you ever seen a player get their shot blocked at the free throw line? Then, why do you have your players start so high? No one can block a shot at the line." A player needs to begin a free throw no higher than their shoulders and chest. It can never get blocked, and a player has enough strength in this area to be an accurate shooter from the line.

A player can hurt his free throw accuracy by shooting too low as well. Once again it is crucial that a player pauses his shot near the chest when he has stopped his dribble. Despite being one of the greatest players in NBA history (two MVP trophies and four NBA Championship trophies will back me up), Tim Duncan has always struggled from the line. Duncan's biggest problem is that he shoots from his hip and therefore loses the power he needs when shooting free throws. If he would pause near the chest, Duncan would find his percentage would increase noticeably.

USE YOUR TOES

We've already discussed my beliefs regarding bending the knees too much on a jump shot. This slows the shot down and makes the shooter easy to defend. Free-throws are a different matter, however. Because there is no defender running up to alter your shot on a free throw, you can take more time and bend your knees more. Please remember that if you bend your knees too much, your legs will tense similar to a person squatting while weightlifting. There needs to be some flexing of the knees, but also a good amount of toes. A free-throw needs lift from the lower body, which requires the knees and toes working together. If either of these areas does not work properly, the shot will generally be short.

REASONS FOR MISSING AT THE LINE:

Young and inexperienced players miss at the free throw line because of shooting release and focus. In other words, many miss simply because they do not put their finger through the rim.

High school players through the professional ranks miss free throws due to another reason altogether. The demon here can be found in the shoulder and neck region. I would estimate 70% of free throws that are missed from ages 15 and up is because the player is tensing the shoulders and neck region. When this occurs you will see misses short and long.

Players here need to relax their shoulders and sway them back. Unlike the jump shot, however, you can not sway the shoulders by leading with your feet. Of course if you did you would go over the line every time for a violation. Once again make sure you are breathing, relax your shoulders and sway them so they do not point straight to the ceiling. If you allow yourself to make these changes, you will dramatically raise your free throw percentage.

GETTING TO THE LINE

If you are a great free throw shooter but you never seem to get to the line, then you have a wasted talent. I have seen free throw shooters that practice their skills and have the shot down to a flawless science but because they are not aggressive, they never get to the line. The most aggressive players attack the basket and get fouled. They are fearless and at times, risks takers. During the 1983-84 season, Adrian Dantley, an All-Star forward for the Utah Jazz, took 946 free throw attempts which projected to 12 per game. Not too bad for a player listed at only 6'4". While he didn't have great size, height, or jumping ability, Dantley had a smooth perimeter jumper and a fearless demeanor to him which allowed him to live at the free throw line.

TO TURN OR NOT TO TURN

While we encourage each player to turn when they are shooting a jump shot, it is up to the player to determine if they want to turn at the line. I always tell players to try the ten toes to basket and then try the turn and see what best works best. The NBA players that noticeably turn when shooting freethrows include: Kobe Bryant, Dwayne Wade, Jameer Nelson and Carmelo Anthony to name a few.

LAST THOUGHTS FROM THE STRIPE

Good free throw shooters must work on their skills everyday from the line. I remember watching Dylan Rigdon stay after each practice and shoot his 100 free throws before going home. He always knew what his consecutive record without a miss was and always tried to break it each time he stepped foot on the hardwood. One night I was rebounding for him at Marina High School and the streak reached 176 consecutively. Great free throw shooters strive for perfection and this method of shooting allows players to reach for new excellence.

CHAPTER 17 WRAP UP:

- Good free throw shooting takes countless hours of practice to master the mental and physical skills.
- Proper free throw accuracy needs to start with technique.
- A quality free throw shooter ALWAYS does the same repetitive motions every single time.
- The first thing any shooter should do as they approach the line is to find the free throw center (the dot).
- Once you receive the ball from the referee, you must take the same amount of dribbles on each free throw.
- Staring at the rim does not help you at the line one bit when dribbling at the line.
- Establish a breathing pattern.
- After taking your dribbles (the same amount every time), you need to effectively pause your shot into your shooting pocket.

18. VISUALIZATION

"Not only does a visualized experience condition the human brain, but it will also program the human body."
Judd Blaslotto
Ph.D., World-Class Power Lifter/Author

As strange as it might seem, the brain can't comprehend the difference between reality and fantasy. Close your eyes and think about shooting a perfect jump shot for five minutes. Now open your eyes. Does your shot feel improved? You have just actually practiced five minutes worth of quality shooting. While your brain is a complex device, it is not smart enough to fully understand the difference when you physically shoot and when you mentally think of shooting.

Are you still a non-believer? Perhaps this will help you understand the significance of proper visualization. The University of Chicago reported an experiment in the effects of mental practice on improving skills in free throw shooting. One group of students actually practiced free throwing every day for 20 days. They were scored on the first and last day. A second group was scored on the first and last day, and engaged in no sort of practice in between. They were told to go home and not shoot and do not even think about basketball. A third group was scored on the first day, and then spent 20 minutes a day imagining that they were shooting at a basket.

The first group, which actually practiced 20 minutes every day, improved 24%. The second group which had no practice, showed no improvement. The third group, which only practiced visualization in their imaginations, improved 23%!

Now that you realize the full importance of visualization, you need to understand what true visualization actually is. It first should be noted that visualization not only works in shooting and basketball, but for all sports. Visualization in athletics was first attempted in a team concept in the United States with the 1976 Olympic Ski Team. Skiers visualized themselves skiing through the course and clearly imagined each bump and turn. The team recorded an overall strong performance and set a benchmark for future Olympic athletes concerning visualization.

Visualization is an easy tool to utilize. When you think about it, we use our imaginations every day. When we are youngsters we are constantly using our creative mind by daydreaming. As we get older, however, we lose much of this imagination. We have to get back to our childhood instincts while adding a dose of discipline to properly visualize as we attempt to improve our shooting. The player must create a series of flawless images that are visual (how it looks), kinesthetic (how the body feels during the motion) and auditory (how the net sounds, the roar of the crowd). These images need to be repetitively played in the mind.

Proper visualizing requires an athlete to be vivid and detailed for it to be effective. Visualization is similar to a highlight film that shows only positive plays and moves.

When visualizing a jump shot, the player needs to have a clear image of what he is imagining and make sure he is always thinking in a constructive manner. This visualization must have the correct behavior, however. Visualizing incorrect behavior will actually damage a player's overall performance.

"THE POW AND VISUALIZATION"

One of my favorite visualization stories concerns a true event that happened during the Viet Nam War. United States Major James Nesmeth was captured by the Viet Cong and was imprisoned in a cage four-and-a-half feet tall and five feet long. During his incarceration, Major Nesmeth was not allowed to do any physical activities nor talk to anyone.

The Major, an avid golfer, thought about golf for 1-2 hours a day. He would close his eyes and visualize what the perfect swing felt like. He envisioned the course and the smell of the grass. He would think about how the perfect putt felt over and over again.

Seven years later Major Nesmeth was freed. Of course as soon as he was well enough he found a golf course. Much to his surprise, the first time he walked on the course he shot 20 strokes below his average. Yes, 20 strokes! He discovered he had become a much better golfer than before he was captured because of his daily visualization techniques.

CHAPTER 18 WRAP UP:

- Your brain is not smart enough to understand the difference when you physically shoot and when you mentally think of shooting.
- Visualization is an easy tool to use to improve your shooting.
- The player must create a series of flawless images that are visual (how it looks), kinesthetic (how the body feels during the motion) or auditory (how the net sounds, the roar of the crowd).
- These images need to be played over and over again in the mind.
- Proper visualizing requires an athlete to be vivid and detailed for it to be very effective.
- Visualizing incorrect behavior will hurt a player's overall performance.

19. DAILY SHOOTING PRACTICE

To become a good shooter you must shoot constantly. Don't take days off and expect to come back 100%. If you go on vacation and fail to shoot, chances are quite high that your shot will continue to be on vacation when you return home. As mentioned before, the best shooters feel guilty if they miss just one day of shooting. They realize that a day has gone by where they did not improve their shooting skills. Do you ever feel this emotion when you take a day off?

Almost any rim with do if it's close to 10 feet. Don't be too choosy about your rims. One to two inches too high or too low of ten feet will not throw your shot off. I hear so many complaints from players that they occasionally have to practice their shooting skills outside. Many of the greatest NBA shooters honed their skills on outdoor courts when they were growing up and this didn't seem to affect them one bit. I doubt if Larry Bird or Jerry West had the luxuries of shooting in air-conditioned gyms when they were young. This Southern California mentality amazes me. It can be 80 degrees outside with perfect weather conditions and players will complain that they don't have an indoor gym to shoot in.

The sorriest site is a 40 year old in a recliner wishing that he had practiced harder and more often as a teenager. Is that what you really want? Will you be asking yourself, "Why didn't I spend more time practicing and less time messing around?" Below are tips and ideas to improve your shooting skills. Follow the tips, work hard on your game, and you won't be regretting your lack of commitment twenty years into the future.

HOW SHOULD ONE SHOOT WHEN PRACTICING?

"I believe you can accomplish more in forty-five minutes of practice if you work hard than you can in two hours if you don't train properly."
Jesse Owens
Track and Field Great

Danny Ainge is one of the greatest shooters of all time. After leading BYU to a NCAA Final Four birth in 1980, Ainge took his shooting skills to Boston and helped the Celtics to three World Championships. One day a reporter asked Ainge, "How much do you shoot in the off season?" Most players and coaches probably believe the answer would be at least four to five hours a day. Ainge, however, replied, "Forty-five minutes to an hour. But when I shoot I bust my butt." The concept of quantity over quality is wrong. It is better to shoot in a "game speed" manner for 30 minutes than shoot for four hours without working up a sweat.

Imagine if a sprinter in track and field never works on his sprinting, but instead jogs lethargically for 30 minutes a day. That athlete never works up a sweat and has no idea what it's like to sprint. He enters his first meet with many of the best 100-meter sprinters in the area. Where will that sprinter finish in the meet? Chances are that he will finish dead last because he did not properly train. The same theory can be applied to shooting. If you don't train to go quick and hard when you shoot, you will naturally fail when you try to be fast in a game.

• Work at game situation shots. Don't shoot 25 footers if you can't make a 15 foot shot. This will not help you in the least. Understand who you are and what you need to work on.

• Go hard or go home. I see players all the time go to a basket and simply go through the motions. They don't shoot quickly and they definitely don't go "game speed." While they may make most of their shots in this "petrified" state, they aren't trying to get better. These are the players that never seem to improve, but they will tell everyone that they live on a court. A player should properly warm-up 10-15 minutes with one handed and stationary shooting. Unless this player is going through a serious shooting slump and needs to work out some flaws in his technique, this is all the time a shooter needs to properly warm-up. Now that you have stretched your upper body muscles and your mind, it is time to shoot in a "game speed" manner.

• Jump when you shoot. Make sure you never stand in one spot. Constantly move and remember to use the balls of your feet and not your heels when shooting.

• Practice with an imagination. Why do some players make 80% of their shots when they're shooting around, but can only make 30% of their shots in games? A large reason lies in that they are practicing the wrong way. In practice they're relaxed and confident. In games they become nervous and feel tension. When they practice by themselves, they don't see other players coming at them to block a shot. In games they hear, see and sometimes feel this nearby defender. Having imagination is very crucial to becoming a first rate shooter. When you're shooting by yourself, imagine as if it's a real game. Try to believe a great defender is closely guarding you. Think as if your next shot is for the league title. Get confidence, be quick, have imagination and focus. Try to see yourself shooting over the best defender in your league on EVERY shot.

• Work on your moves when you are shooting. Few players today work on their up-fakes and jab-steps when practicing in a gym, at the school yard, or in the driveway. Everyone wishes to be a scorer, but how are you going to get these shots off? Why was Larry Bird such a great scorer? Yes, partly because he was an exceptional shooter, but also because he was a master of the shot fake. The better you are at faking the shot, the easier it will be for you to shoot and score. A player should be able to mix the drive, the short pull-up jumper and the outside jumper when working out.

• Play 1-on-1. Very few players play 1-on-1 anymore. Maybe that's why few individuals have good moves and know what to do once a player is guarding them. Playing 1-on-1 greatly helps players to learn to shoot with a hand in the face. When playing one-on-one, make sure you also have structured rules which include three dribbles or less. The ball should be checked (reset) after every rebound and use "winner's outs." Lastly, make sure you're taking it serious when you play. I often see players screw around which can cause injury or a lack of improvement. Play to win! If you have three players, play one-on-one-on one. If played correctly, it's a great competitive game.

20. TAKING THE LAST SHOT

"It's interesting to watch how some players want the ball and others want to run away from the ball. Some players can score 45 or 50 points then suddenly disappear when the game is on the line."
Billy Cunningham,
Basketball Hall of Fame Player

Few players want to take the game winning shot. For the most part, most of them don't want to be responsible for letting their team down if they miss the last shot. There are, however, a few individuals that don't worry about making or missing the last shot and always look forward to taking the game winner.

Jerry West was dubbed the nickname Mr. Clutch for all of his last minute heroics. Michael Jordan was notorious for miraculously saving games from the jaws of defeat with last second winning shots. Reggie Miller and Robert Horry (see picture) also are superb clutch performers. Perhaps the newest member to this "ice in our veins" fraternity is Kobe Bryant. What sets these players apart from the rest of their teammates and players in their league is that they thoroughly enjoy pressure situations and believe in themselves. Most of these players visualize themselves succeeding and never consider failing or missing a last second shot. Speaking of visualizing, most great clutch basketball performers practiced their last second shooting heroics growing up. They would play mind games with themselves by creating the image that a top-notch defender is blanketed on them with time running out. Through years of hard work, this one time fantasy now has become reality.

"I JUST SHOOT THE BALL"

During the 2003/2004 basketball season I coached the Fountain Valley Boys' High School Team. We were not the most talented team, nor the tallest, strongest or quickest, but we did possess a "scrappy" style of play that allowed us to post a 21-4 mark and a Sunset League Championship. Mike Almanza was not close to being my leading scorer that season. He would, however, average double figures in scoring and become an effective three-point shooter.

Mike's biggest asset to our team was that he possessed an uncanny knack of hitting the big shot late in a game. During that season, Mike made five shots in the last 10 seconds that either became the game winning shot or one that tied the contest and sent it into overtime. If we wouldn't have had Mike that season, we would not have won our two tournament championships and league title. I asked him one time after practice, "Mike, how do you do it? How do you consistently hit the big shot?"

Mike shrugged his shoulders and smiled, "Coach, I don't know. I just shoot the ball." What Mike didn't fully comprehend is that the reason he was such a pressure shooter was because he never thought about the importance of each shot. Great "clutch" players shoot the ball and take the last shot with the same lack of pressure as if they are attempting the first shot of the game.

CAN YOU HANDLE THE PRESSURE?

"I know that I do things down the stretch without even thinking about them. Then I'll go back and see the game on film and say, 'Damn, that was a big shot I made. I can't believe I took it.' "
Larry Bird
Basketball Hall of Fame Player

The players that handle pressure well never think of missing or making. They don't hear the little voice inside the head that is always informing the player of the consequences of the shot ("You better make this one—it's important"). They focus, relax, and shoot. They tune everything else out including crowd distractions.

While the process of pressurized shooting is to focus on the task and not to be overly concerned about the importance of the shot, it is also imperative for the player to want the ball late in a game. You can not be the clutch player if you do not have the ball. Clutch performers not only want the ball, but they expect it and often times demand it.

BEING "THE MAN"

"The difference between an average player and a great player is confidence."
Charles Barkley
Basketball Hall of Fame Player

Becoming a team's "go-to" player and having the confidence to propel that squad to victory by taking the last shot of a game does not come instantly. First and foremost, the player must have skills. If you can't hit a shot while scrimmaging in practice, why would you think you could make it when the game (not to mention the season) is on the line? If you look at the best players in college and the professional ranks, they all have obvious skills. Many of the best all-time basketball players are also some of the greatest pressure players.

There's more to it, however, than just having skills. Not every talented player can be counted on late in a game to hit the game winning shot. He must first and foremost believe in himself and the notion that he will succeed. If you asked Reggie Miller in a timeout, "Reggie, are you going to make this game winning shot?" He would look at you as if you've lost your mind and would respond, "Of course." In Reggie Miller's mind and the mindset of all clutch shooters, failure never occurs. I've actually seen clutch players become surprised when they miss a game winning shot because they can't ever conceive the notion of failing.

Obviously if a player is going to shoot the last shot he must have confidence in his overall abilities, especially in his shooting skills. Very rarely will an NBA player take a game winning shot that lacks confidence. First of all, if he lacks confidence, he will probably be sitting on the bench and would not be in the game for the most significant possessions. Secondly, the coach will never draw up a play for the player (or as a second or third option) if that player doesn't believe in himself.

THE NEW MR. CLUTCH

"I never look at the consequences of missing a big shot...
when you think about the consequences you
always think of a negative shot."
Michael Jordan
Hall of Fame Player

Michael Jordan is conceivably the most clutch athlete during the last century. His legacy began in the 1982 NCAA Finals as Jordan, only a freshman, hit a 20-foot baseline jumper to propel North Carolina over Georgetown, 52-50. Jordan built his legacy through time by successfully nailing game winning shots.

Jordan's most famous shot, however, became the last shot he took in a Chicago Bulls uniform. On June 14, 1998 the Bulls played the Utah Jazz in Game 6 of the NBA Finals. Two days earlier Jordan had missed a last second shot to give the Jazz new life and send the series back to Utah. Most players sulk about missing the shot that gave home court advantage back to your opponents. With Jordan, however, this miss gave him additional motivation. Here were Jordan's comments after the Game 5 miss: "I love those moments. Great players thrive on that because they have an opportunity to decide happiness and sadness. That's what you live for. That's the fun part about it."

Jordan didn't feel sorry for himself or think about what might have been, however. He took this miss in stride by realizing there would be another game that he'd be counted on to make the game winning shot. That other game would take place less than 48 hours later at the Salt Palace in Salt Lake City. In Game 6 the Jazz had the momentum for a good majority of the game. The Bulls, however, would never say die as they continued to stay close with the Jazz. Down 86-85 with only 20 seconds left, Jordan stole the ball and set up for the last shot. With Jazz defender, Bryon Russell closely guarding him, Jordan surveyed the scene. In two previous NBA Championship Series clinching moments for the Bulls, Jordan was looked upon as the decoy. Because of potential double teams, he became the passer—to John Paxson (1993 vs. the Phoenix Suns) for a three-pointer and Steve Kerr (1997 vs. the Utah Jazz) for an 18 foot jumper—instead of the finisher. This game, however, would put the spotlight directly back on Jordan. With time running down, Russell slightly reached which made him lose his footing for a brief instant. "When Russell reached, I took advantage of the moment," Jordan commented after the game. "I never doubted myself. I never doubted the whole game." Jordan seized the moment as he pulled-up and sank the 15 footer to give the Bulls an 87-86 victory and their sixth NBA Championship in eight years.

The great players always want to be in the game during the pressure packed moments. They want to be able to decide the outcomes of games, series, and often times the entire season. These clutch performers usually have outstanding skills, courage, and of course confidence. They are never afraid to fail and always want the ball late in a game. Players that lack skills and an overall belief in themselves won't even get close to the ball as the clock ticks down. They don't want to be responsible for deciding the outcome of a game, let alone an entire season. As you continue on further, you will read about how players become great and the different steps it takes. You must understand that greatness and being a clutch performer are very much related. You can't do one without the other.

CHAPTER 20 WRAP UP:

- What sets the great clutch players apart from the rest of their teammate is that they thoroughly enjoy pressure and believe in themselves. Most of these players visualize themselves as always succeeding and usually never think about failing.

- Most players do not want to take the game winning shot.

- Most great clutch performers in basketball practiced their last second shooting growing up.

- Great "clutch" players shoot the ball and take the last shot of a game with the same lack of pressure as if they are attempting the first shot of the game.

21. SHOOTING DRILLS

"It's not how good you are. It's how good you can be."
Kevin McHale
Basketball Hall of Fame Player

Now that you understand what you are supposed to do, I will give you drills that will get you to the "promise land" for shooters. Many of these drills will be difficult at first to perform, but if you practice in a diligent and focused manner you will notice each day the drills will become easier and your shot will become more accurate. These drills are broken down into three facets: STRENGTH, ACCURACY, and SPEED. All three aspects are important and need to be practiced at least 4-5 times a week.

STRENGTH DRILLS

An attribute that I learned from Coach Ed is that great jump shooters have strong hands. Thankfully, he introduced me to the on ball pushup. Many of these other strength drills I developed over a course of time.

ON BALL PUSHUPS--This is terrific for building up your hand and arm strength. This drill is more difficult than regular pushups. Ten on ball pushups equals to 30 regular pushups. Do as many as you can without stopping. If you are not strong enough to do an on ball pushup, then stay in a stance similar to the picture on the right for at least 30 seconds until you become stronger.

TWO BALL PUSHUPS—This works out the triceps and hand strength as well as your chest muscles. Attempt to do a minimum of 10 two ball pushups. If you are advanced, go until exhaustion hits.

CHEVY BOUNCING DRILLS—Get into a on ball pushup position stance with your arms completely outstretched. Attempt to lift the ball up in an up and down position. You can do this in a limited stationary space or going forward 10-30 yards. You will definitely feel it in your hands and chest.

SPEED DRILLS

JUMPING ROPE— Many of my best shooters are strong advocates of jump roping, and I strongly encourage all my students to jump rope as much as they can. Most students don't like to jump rope because it's boring, however. Use the following as training tips with the jump rope:

- Don't just jump rope to jump rope. Be creative, disciplined and work hard. Combine jumping rope in a limited space with overall distance. Every player should jump rope a minimum of 5-10 minutes a day. Make sure when you jump rope for distance you go a minimum of 30 yards.

- Don't jump rope in a boring manner. Be creative. Listen to music while jumping rope. It helps to pass time.

- It seems as if everyone has a jump rope, but no one ever uses it a consistent basis. I ask my students, "Where's your jump rope?" The response is usually, "It's in my garage" or "in my closet." Get it out. Collecting dust is all the jump rope is good for in those locations.

- Carry your jump rope in your gym bag and use it on a daily basis.

CONE/HURDLE WORK—As I have mentioned before, proper jump shooting is a plyometric exercise from the waist down. Five years ago I introduced plyometric exercises with shooting and quickly saw immediate results with my students. By focusing on the toes and giving each player more spring, most of the players' shots became remarkably quicker. A good majority of this plyometric work is done with mini plastic cones or plyometric hurdles.

SINGLE CONE/HURDLE JUMPS—When using the cones it is important to remember that you should "be quick, but not in a hurry" where you actually become panicked. Get a cone/hurdle and use it in the following ways:

- Hop over the side (both left and right)
- Hop over going forward
- Hop over going side and then back

TRIPLE CONES/HURDLES JUMPING FORWARD—Line up three cones/hurdles and jump over them into your shot. Please remember that your feet should be light and that each hop should be the same in height and speed. This drill can be used inside and outside of the three point shot.

TRIPLE CONES/HURDLES JUMPING SIDEWAYS—This is similar to the three cones/hurdles forward with of course the cones are now to the side. Make sure you can either go outside to inside and then reverse the pattern. It is important in this drill to challenge yourself and put the cones in unusual positions especially if you have conquered the normal angles.

REGGIE MILLER DRILL—The king of the three point shot, Reggie Miller does this drill as the clock ticks down before every game. He will always be at the top of the key and will watch the clock as it counts down. Right before the buzzer, he will stand facing the other basket, turn into a hop and do a complete 180 degree shot. This is excellent to develop quicker feet.

OVER CONE ON PULLUP—This is an outstanding drill in developing quicker feet and a faster pull-up jump shot. Begin out on the perimeter well past the three point line. Practice your pull-up only this time you must hurdle over a cone with both feet. As you bounce down you will come immediately back up ready to shoot the ball. Please remember that the longer you are on the ground on your first bounce, the slower your shot will take.

BACKWARDS HOPS—Start at or near the block facing the basket. Hop three times backwards with quick and rhythmic bounces. Make sure all three hops are exactly the same. After hoping the third time, shoot the ball in a relaxed manner. This helps not only your lower body speed, but also relaxing your shoulders. Make sure on this drill that you do not fight your shoulders, but instead let the shoulders take control of your shot. This drill can be used for the Natural fade, the Big Fade or the Leaner.

BLOCK TO CORNER—Start on a block at the key with your back to the basket. Now take one dribble to the opposite corner of the free throw line. Make sure you are working on the hop on this drill and not the 1-2 Step. The dribble must be long and while in the air make sure you are turning to square up. Focus also on the quick bounce and the spring in your toes.

ACCURACY DRILLS

ONE HANDED SHOOTING—As already mentioned, one of the best drills that you can possibly do is one handed shooting. Of all the drills in this chapter I recommend this the most. It helps with extension and keeping the ball straight. Make sure when you attempt this that you start in an L position simply because you are only shooting with one hand. If you start in a V position one handed, the ball will incorrectly roll right off the hand. Start in close and as you get warm start working your way further back.

ONE HANDED SHOOTING AGAINST BACKBOARD SIDE—Another drill is shooting against the side of a backboard. Because for warming this is a narrow object, this drill can be beneficial for overall shooting accuracy. Line up about 5-8 feet away from the side of the backboard and shoot one handed. Always hold your follow through until the ball hits the ground. You should aim right above the padding.

CHAIR SHOOTING—Sit back in a chair, relax and shoot. This drill will greatly help assist your overall strength and your shoulders will experience less tension. By sitting back in the chair, your shoulders automatically become relaxed. This is a first-rate drill for players that are constantly tense. You may want to do this drill with a partner. If you attempt this drill without a partner, you will have to stand up and retrieve the ball quite often.

LARRY BIRD SHOOTING—This drill is designed for two players which includes a passer/rebounder and a shooter. The shooter should stand 10-15 feet from the basket. The passer must give accurate passes and the shooter will catch and shoot the ball without jumping. Everything here is focusing on upper body techniques, which includes the release.

SHOOTING ON BACK—This is a great drill to do, especially if the player has no basket to practice on. Make sure that when you do this that the focus always remains on your release. Too often the player that does this drill only focuses on the ball and actually picks up bad habits. Make sure that you focus on the release, especially your index finger. Don't worry about the ball.

SHOOTING WITHOUT A BALL—As I have revealed many times throughout Pro Shooting Secrets, repetition is crucial for overall shooting success. One of the best drills to improve muscle memory is shooting without a basketball. Make sure that you don't just go through the motions, however. Every shot that you shoot without a basketball should be done correctly.

ARM EXTENSIONS—Extend your arm into a locked position while placing the ball in your shooting hand. Stand five feet away from the basket and now try shooting. Flexing your knees and using toes will greatly help. This drill will help you to strengthen your wrist.

FINGER FOCUS— This is a very unique drill that forces a player to focus on his release. Turn your feet to the side. For right handed players they should turn to the left side and left handed players should turn to the right. Most coaches would look at this drill and believe we are actually teaching not being squared. What we are doing in this drill is focusing on putting the finger through the rim. In other words, this becomes a focus and aiming drill.

DEFENDER SHOOTING—Have a defensive player with the ball standing under the basket. The offensive player will stand out at the three point line. The defensive player passes to the offensive player and attempts to block or alter the shooter. This is a basic, but important drill so a player gets used to shooting with a defender flying at him. After awhile have the offensive player be able to also use the up fake and the pull-up as well. Make sure the defensive player is working hard in this drill. When a player shoots he should follow the rebound and now he becomes the passer.

22. THE PURE SHOOTER

"Don't you know that you are a shooting star.
And all the world will love you Just as long as you are."
Bad Company
From the Song, "Shooting Star"

After you begin shooting consistently in a focused manner, your next goal is to become a pure shooter. To be a "perfect" shooter you have to obviously put in more time than the "novice" shooter who may shoot only on weekends. Alan Lambert, writer for The Basketball Highway, wrote, "It is estimated for most basketball skills that it takes 250,000 nearly perfect repetitions to automate a skill." To get to this total a player would have to shoot 500-600 shots every other day a week for over two years.

Besides repetition, this shooting stage is also based around perfection, the number game, and extension. In the process you will break shooting rules and beliefs developed during the past 50 years. Very few players ever become pure shooters often because they don't have any notion of advanced shooting concepts.

A pure shooter's mindset is drastically different than average shooters. A pure shooter is a true artist always trying to hone and perfect his craft. An average shooter usually has a lethargic attitude towards shooting. For most average shooters, shooting is just a single facet of basketball. On the other hand, pure shooters take great pride in their shooting abilities. The pure shooter's attitude is very similar to a gunslinger from the old west. A pure shooter understands that his shooting abilities will distinctively separate him from his teammates and the opposition.

Today's pure shooters have altered the old gunslinger battle cry of "Have gun will travel" to "Have shot will travel." Despite being a step slow or often times being vertically challenged, a pure shooter not only can have a solid high school career, but also may have an opportunity to earn a college scholarship because of his marksman talents. Pure shooter, Kurt Oliver (considered one of my finest shooters that I have instructed), would earn a college scholarship despite barely being able to touch the rim.

Pure shooters are also known for their longevity. The shot is always the last thing to falter on an elite shooter. Because all NBA teams always need experienced shooters on their rosters, you will often see pure shooters that will play well into their thirties (a few examples of this are: Steve Kerr, Reggie Miller and Glen Rice). Good athletes that lack shooting skills last only as long their legs remain at 100%. Once their quickness skills start deteriorating, their playing days become numbered.

PERFECTION

If you wish to become a pure shooter and you are currently a good shooter, your next step is to seek shooting perfection. For poor to average shooters the ultimate goal becomes making the shot. As you enter the pure shooting stage, however, the shooter now should expect all of his shots to end in a swish. The thought process here is that if you swish in practice, you will almost certainly make the shot in a game.

THE NUMBERS GAME

To enter into the pure shooting stage you must start playing mental games with yourself. The mental games which I'm speaking about never include negative or positive emotions. Instead these become short term goals that are comprised of numbers. For instance, take ten shots from a certain area and give yourself a number that you need to make. These numbers can be different depending on distance and degree of difficulty. If you're working on your pull-up jump shot you might want to start with having to make 7 out of 10 shots. Once you master this number on a regular basis, increase it to 8 and then later to 9.

This training concept helps you to fully understand where you are as a shooter, while giving yourself goals to shoot for. Average shooters just shoot and never have a goal in mind. Pure shooters are always trying to get better and understand how important the mental side of shooting can be.

Once you set your goals, keep documented records of your shooting. When shooting by yourself, keep records that include date, how many you made and attempted, and the shooting percentage. Make sure you include records of shooting off the dribble as well as off the pass. With daily focused practice, you will notice your shooting percentages will improve with time.

EXTENSION AND ANGLES

To become a pure shooter you need to not only extend but also work on your angles. Obviously the tougher the angle, the tougher the shot becomes. I truly believe working on angles and extension for pure shooters is like running on the beach. If you have ever tried to run on sand you will know how difficult it can be. As soon as you step foot on a solid surface you quickly notice how much easier it is to walk or run. When you reach this elite level of shooting and then work on difficult shots, shooting a wide open shot becomes so much easier.

Angles are very similar to the "extension shot" with the only difference being you are normally going in the opposite direction with your dribble. Quite often you will start with your back to the basket. Creativity is very important here as you will develop many different angles with time. Working on your angles will also greatly help you in developing foot speed especially in coming off screens.

BREAKING THE RULES

"If you want to shoot like Kobe Bryant, then you should shoot like Kobe Bryant. If you wish to be a pure shooter, then don't shoot like 10 year old Bobby from the Y."

Paul Hoover
Pro Shot Shooting System Founder

Pure shooters do not employ the North American shooting methods that are currently being taught: squaring the feet, knees bent, back straight and starting the shot above the head. This looks less like Phoenix Sun's sharpshooter, Steve Nash and more like a seizure. To become a top notch shooter needs to go away from these old fashioned theories and focus on squaring the shooting shoulder, using the balls of feet, relaxing the neck and shoulders, and being a one eyed shooter.

Pure shooters can get their shot off at any time thanks in large part to the fade away, the step back, the runner, and the leaner. My greatest challenge is often times the coach of the player that I'm instructing. As I have mentioned before coaches were taught by their coaches who were taught by their coaches. In other words, many times the shooting methods that they are using are from the basketball prehistoric days well before the three point shot. Basketball has changed greatly in just the past decade alone, let alone the last fifty years.

Constantly I hear the comment from young athletes, "But my coach would never let me shoot that way." From coaches I hear, "That's okay for Ray Allen to shoot that way, but little Johnny can never do that." Is Ray Allen such a great shooter because he broke the shooting "rules" at a young age OR is it because he is RAY ALLEN and because he is such a great shooter he can break the shooting rules. While I realize some basketball observers may disagree, I believe it's the first choice.

LET FREEDOM RING!!

Coach Mike Krzyzewski once wrote, "If you put a plant in a jar, it will take the shape of that jar. But if you allow the plant to grow freely, twenty jars might not be enough to hold it." I believe the same concept goes for players especially shooters. If you don't allow players to show some freedom when shooting, they will never grow. If you allow players to create their own shot and use the fade, they will prosper and grow. You could see this first hand with Krzyzewski's coaching of JJ Redick. Redick, the all-time leading scorer at Duke, was able to thrive and break records thanks to Coach K's encouragement and freedom.

THE PLAYER BECOMES THE TEACHER

Jeff Hornacek is one of the best pure shooters to ever play in the NBA. A 15 year NBA veteran, Hornacek grew up as a scrawny player competing against older players on the playground. Having a difficult time getting his shot off in the traditional shooting style, he would put fades and leans into his repertoire which greatly helped his offensive production.

Desert News sports columnist Doug Robinson writes, "It isn't just that Hornacek could shoot accurately that raised eyebrows; it's that he could do it from so many angles and in so many ways – falling away, leaning, looking the other way, over 7-footers, under 7 footers, half-hooks, running jumpers, underhand, overhand, whatever —and all of them with the quickest release in the NBA. When necessary, he actually shots the ball at the same time he was catching it. It's as if Hornacek has a microchip in his brain, which, in a split second, calculates distance, angle, body lean, trajectory needed to clear a defender's hands, precise ETA of the in-coming defender and the latest possible launch time allowable to beat the block. He sees things in slow motion, which allowed him to pick apart defenders and defenses. All of this compensated for any lack of jumping ability and speed. His shot was rarely blocked, even though he often ventured into the lane. The first time Hornacek faced Ralph Sampson, the 7-foot-4 sensation; he took the ball right at him twice and flipped the ball into the basket over Sampson's outstretched arms.

Nothing Hornacek did was unpracticed or uncalculated. He practiced those shots, or something close to them, and if he hadn't then, that computer in his brain did the rest. He studied and honed his shot, as well. Hornacek kept a notebook in which he recorded details and observations about his shooting technique and then referred to them when he hit the rare slump.

When he first came into the league, Hornacek was reluctant to attempt his unorthodox shots, such as his signature running jumper, because he was uncertain how coaches would respond. According to all standards of technique, a shooter should check his body's drift and take a balanced shot. Hornacek thought otherwise, and eventually coaches not only accepted it, they asked him how he did it and began teaching it to others."

Jeff Hornacek, like countless other pure shooters in the NBA and in college, learned to break traditional rules for an opportunity at shooting greatness. Hornacek became a great shooter through hard work and discipline, but also because he opened his mind to go where only a few shooters have ever traveled.

CHAPTER 22 WRAP UP:

- The pure shooting stage is based around perfection, the number game, and extension. In the process you will break shooting rules and beliefs developed over 50 years ago.
- As you enter the pure shooting stage the shooter now should expect all of his shots to end in a swish.
- To enter into the pure shooting stage you also must start playing mental games with yourself.

23. MYTHS AND LIES OF SHOOTING

1. SQUARING UP—When you ask most coaches to name the most important element of shooting they often times will answer, "Squaring up to the basket." These coaches will remind their players each day to square up with their feet. In return these coaches produce players that will always be struggling with their shoulders due to too much tension. Once again it is important to focus on squaring up the player's dominant shooting shoulder to the basket and NOT the feet.

2. FOUR FINGERS DOWN—Very few coaches and players understand the importance of the index finger when shooting. Their normal response is to snap the wrist and use all four fingers when shooting. This flawed technique will make you into a inconstant shooter at best. Snapping your follow-through with four fingers down will cause your shot to miss to the left and right.

3. BEND YOUR KNEES—This is possibly the biggest myth in all of sports. The more you bend, the slower your shot becomes. If you bend too much, you actually lose power in your shot. Remember to always FLEX your knees, but do not bend them.

4. SHOOT STRAIGHT UP AND DOWN—Coaches use this often so their players won't attempt to fade. Shooting a basketball or doing any activity in sports is impossible by going straight up and down. The shoulders and neck will tense, which forces the shot to become spastic.

5. THINKING OF NOTHING WHEN YOU SHOOT—This may be correct if you're a NBA three point specialist, but if you're a young player attempting to get shooting fundamentals and accuracy down, I strongly advise against this. If you are a young shooter and think of nothing when you shoot, your shot will generally have no discipline and the release will be inconsistent at best.

6. THINKING OF MAKING IT WHEN YOU SHOOT—The worst shooters in the world think about making it when they shoot. While it is important to be positive when shooting, a player needs to focus on the process and not the outcome. Coaches often tell their players, "Be positive and think of making it." In reality, this is the worst thing they can think about.

7. GO MEET THE PASS—You should only go meet the pass when you are being tightly guarded. If you go meet a pass with extended hands, when you're open, you will either have to bring the ball back into your shooting pocket or you will bring the ball back to your head in a "Hitch" shot. Both take too much time and the "Hitch" forces your shot into a throwing motion.

8. ALWAYS USE THE 1-2 STEP—This is the lower body form that is universally taught through youth and high school levels, and yet less than 20% of all shots in the NBA are from "1-2 Step" technique. My biggest problem with this form is that it generally lacks speed and overall rhythm. There are times to use the "1-2 Step" when shooting, but it should never be the "cure-all" remedy for lower body shooting.

9. FOCUSING ON THE FRONT OF THE RIM OR THE BACK OF THE RIM—If you focus on the front or back of the rim, chances are you will hit these spots.

Most great shooters focus on the middle of the rim. After all, if you want the ball to go through the middle of the rim, shouldn't you focus in that area?

10. BACKSPIN IS IMPORTANT—Physics tests have confirmed that backspin is only important if the ball hits the rim. The backspin gives it a soft touch to roll in. According to some coaches, this is one of the most important elements of being a pure shooter. While I would rather have my shooters have proper backspin, I do believe there are many more crucial aspects in making a shot than backspin.

11. SHOOTING THE SAME WAY EVERY TIME—Coaches will constantly claim that each shot should be the same when practicing. This belief, however, is half true and half false. When a player shoots the release hand and the off hand are usually always in the same location and should always be doing the same action each time. Everything else after that can change depending on where the defender is, the quality of the defender (does he have long arms? Is he quick?), location on the floor, and the shot and game clock. Often times a quality shooter will have to use a big fade on his shot because the clock is ready to expire. If you have never worked on a big fade, you will miss terribly.

12. STARTING POINT IS L AND ABOVE THE HEAD—The higher you begin your shot, the harder it becomes to accurately shoot. As you increase your starting point on your shot, you decrease your overall strength. The shot also greatly slows down when you begin your shot too high.

13. ALWAYS FOLLOW YOUR SHOT—From the age we first shoot we are told by our coaches to always follow our shots. Many players are so consumed by this that as soon as thy shoot they run after their shot. By doing so, they forget to properly hold their follow-through. While it is important to follow your shot, don't be consumed by it. It can actually do great damage to your shot.

24. THE LAST WORDS

"It's Showtime Folks."
Roy Scheider as Joe Gideon
From the Motion Picture, "All That Jazz."

Now that you have nearly completed this book, you should be ready to take your newly acquired knowledge and skills to the gyms and show your teammates and coaches what comprises a quality shooter. Remember, great shooters are not born, but they are created through time. Understand that in the first few months you will have games where you can't miss and then there will be other moments that you can't seem to make a shot. You may momentarily fail, but also realize that you must always learn from these failures.

"KNOWING ALL THE ANSWERS"

As I have mentioned before, I taught freshmen English at John Muir High School during the 1996/97 school year. Twice a month I would give my students a fill in the blanks 40 questions test. This exam took place on a Friday and two days prior I disclosed to each class what exactly was going to be on the forthcoming exam. When attending high school, I was known for studying the wrong notes and focusing too hard on portions of chapters that never appeared on tests. I never wanted this to happen to my students. Therefore, I provided my students with the exact questions and answers that would be on the upcoming test. Despite knowing every question and answer on the test, I would still have 40% of the class fail these exams.

My question to you is: Are you similar to these apathetic students when it comes to shooting? Don't laugh at this comparison. Remember I have given you all the questions and answers for total shooting success. When in doubt, you should remember the answer to end all answers—"finger through the rim.

Make sure you refer to this book if you get into a shooting slump. Never panic, but instead remain calm and ask yourself, "What am I doing wrong?" and then, "How can I properly fix it?" Make sure the negative thoughts remain out of your shot and you focus on ways to correct your errors. Understand that in all my years of training, I have never made any of my students into a quality shooter. I have HELPED EACH PLAYER become a great shooter, but ultimately it is up to each student to decide the discipline, focus, and overall commitment he wishes to set forth in shooting. You have the information in this book to become a first-rate shooter. If you are reading this chapter, then hopefully this means you have also read through the previous chapters and understand where you need to go and the knowledge that you need to take with you to properly get you there. NOW GO DO IT!

I often explain to my students that knowledge is very similar to a baton in a relay race. As a teacher, I pass this knowledge onto each of my students. Each student then must decide if he should accept this knowledge (like the baton) and run with it OR drop it and reject it. If you drop the baton in the Olympics you become disqualified and the race that you've trained endless hours for is suddenly over. If my student decides to accept and run with it, his shooting possibilities are endless. If they drop the knowledge and decide not to use it, they may have future problems in accurate shooting.

"THE FISHERMAN"

Many people think I'm a shooting coach, where in reality I'm actually much closer to a skilled fisherman. Everyday I go to work, cast my line out and see how many individuals I hook. Thirty-three percent of my students ignore the bait entirely. They don't want to try to learn to shoot correctly. These are the players that always fail to improve their shooting.

Thirty-three percent of my students nibble on the bait. In other words, they pick out only out what they want to hear. These players usually improve a little bit.

Lastly, thirty-three percent of my students swallow the bait completely. They listen to everything I say, go home and practice and come back greatly improved. Obviously these are the players that I thoroughly enjoy working with. After reading Pro Shooting Secrets, you need to ask yourself, "Which fish am I?"

You now have the knowledge of a great shooter. Make sure you strive for greatness and don't settle to be second best. With a quick and accurate shot your whole life on a basketball court will suddenly flourish.

"And Charlie—don't forget what happened to the man who suddenly got everything he'd ever wished for."
Willie Wonka

"What happened?"
Charlie Bucket

"He lived happily ever after."
Willie Wonka

From the motion picture, "Willie Wonka and the Chocolate Factory"

25. ACKNOWLEDGEMENTS

"Basketball is sharing."
Phil Jackson
Eleven Time Head Coach of NBA Champions

First and foremost, I would like to greatly thank my parents, Henry and Jill, for encouraging me in my pursuits on the hardwood. In lean times they have stuck by me and my passion to train young athletes. Without their support, I probably would have moved on to another profession long ago.

A special appreciation needs to be directed to a few of my former students who helped me to comprehend different shooting aspects that helped me to build the Pro Shot System. Irving Chong (shooting alignment), Jamaal Taylor (the off hand), Dylan Rigdon and Mike Hopkins (lower body and "The Hop") helped me to discover shooting facets that few coaches fully understand. I am also indebted to the late Des Flood for the time he spent with me as a young coach. I also appreciate the discussions that I've had with other shooting experts including Craig Hodges, Bill Bayno, Dr. Tom Amberry and Ed Palubinskas.

I would also like to give my gratitude to those that helped edit Pro Shooting Secrets which includes: Veronica Lopez, Mike Mahon, Bonnie White, Gary Jones, Larry Davies, Steven Schultz, and especially Joe Metcalfe.

Lastly, I wish to thank all the players that I have trained and coached over the past 25 years. Hopefully, I inspired you as much as you inspired me. Thank you for your dedication, patience and allowing me to teach you. I'd like to leave with a quote from John Wooden in the poem, "They Ask Me Why I Coach." Coach Wooden's sentiments are very similar to mine. "They ask me why I coach and I reply, where could I find more splendid company?"